*Dedicated to My mother, grandmother and brother
who continue to live each and every day in my heart and soul.*

*To my wife and best friend, Christina who has continued to love
and support me throughout my life and in my dreams.*

*To my son and daughter, Adam and Chelsea, I can never express how
special both of you have been in my life. You have made my life complete.*

*To my friends and family, whose support and enthusiasm
has granted me the freedom to be me.*

Chaos to Balance
A Life-changing Strategy

Raymond Salcido, L.C.S.W.

RaiseMeRight, Inc.

For more information please contact chaosaddiction@msn.com
or visit www.chaostobalance.com

Book design by:
Arbor Books, Inc.
19 Spear Road, Suite 301
Ramsey, NJ 07446
www.arborbooks.com

Printed in the United States of America

Chaos to Balance—A Life-changing Strategy
Raymond Salcido, L.C.S.W.

1. Title 2. Author 3. Self-help/Addiction/Psychology

Library of Congress Control Number: 2008941213

ISBN 10: 0-9822302-0-6
ISBN 13: 978-0-9822302-0-6

Table of Contents

Chapter 1

Discovering Chaos

Fifty-four-year-old Tom Marlin, a successful entrepreneur, is considered by many to be laidback and levelheaded, and his friends count on him for advice, problem solving and fun. But if you were to ask his wife and secretary about him, they would probably tell you there's a whole lot more to the story. In fact, they might suggest that Tom is nothing short of "the master of disaster."

"He can't even go a week without losing an important file," his wife, Sue, informs. "One time, he even lost his paycheck! Of course, his timing is always impeccable. He usually loses something important right before he needs it."

The clincher, according to Sue: He always finds what's missing... eventually. But during the usually frantic search, he tends to (relentlessly) blame Sue or his secretary for misplacing the missing item. By the time he's found what he's looking for, everyone is so irritated with him for being a flake and not taking any responsibility for his own screw-ups that they rarely feel like talking to him anymore.

His typical response: "What's the big deal? I found it, didn't I?"

Nancy Garson, forty-two, a stay-at-home mother of three, admits that she hates to pay unnecessary fees and trumped up service charges.

It's unfortunate, then, that whenever she packs for a weekend getaway, she almost always forgets either her cell phone or its charger. What inevitably ends up happening is that she is forced to call her kids long-distance from the landline in her hotel room. Much to her chagrin, the service charges add up pretty quickly.

Nancy also seems to have an almost pathological inability to take out enough cash before she travels. So she spends a lot of her time walking around strange cities in search of ATMs with low or no service fees. Usually, as she would confess, she gives up and uses the next machine she finds, regardless of how ridiculous its charges may be.

"Then," she says, "when I get my phone bill or bank statement, I call and complain. But you know how rude customer service people can be. I end up feeling totally ripped off."

Friends of real estate agent Barry Janus joke that he's the ultimate drama king. Ask how his day is going and you'll hear some variation of his soap opera life. Here's just one example:

He's late to an important appointment because he gets a flat tire after parking in a pile of broken glass that he didn't notice. He finally calls the client to say he's on the way, but misses his exit when he drops his cell phone. Twenty minutes later, he arrives to find a prickly client, and in a moment of "look what a good guy I really am" panic, offers to snag impossible-to-get tickets to a sold-out football game. Thus begins the latest chapter in "As Barry Janus' Life Turns."

"I don't know why I never have any extra money," says twenty-four-year-old Melissa Lowder, who sells health club memberships for a living. But if you look at her sales records, the answer to her predicament is simple: Every time she has a really good month in the commissions department, the next few months go down the tubes. But for Melissa, there are always valid explanations for her regular slumps.

"One month," she explains, "I had the flu for a week. Then, my sister came to visit. Another time, I had to help a coworker with a problem, so I couldn't do my own work. There's always something that seems to pop up and need my attention—immediately!"

More often than not, Melissa only manages to find a way out of her slumps and crank things back into high gear when her bank balance reaches a critical low.

So why discuss these four particular people to kick off the book? The answer lies in the very thing that links them (and indeed links millions of others, as well). While Tom, Nancy, Barry, and Melissa lead vastly different lives, they all have one important thing in common: They display a pattern of chaotic behavior so identifiable, so relatable, and so common that most of us dismiss it as simply flaky, irritating, or melodramatic. After all, who among us doesn't periodically run late, lose something, or procrastinate—even all three at once?

It's not enough to simply state that this self-sabotaging behavior has become so commonplace as to seem almost mundane. Unfortunately, to say that it has reached epidemic proportions might not do it enough justice, either. No, it's far worse than that. In my many years as a practicing psychotherapist, I've discovered more than enough evidence to suggest that this self-sabotaging behavior can be called an *addiction*, one that requires treatment as aggressive as detox.

These days, more and more people come into my office addicted to chaos. They're typical corporate executives, sullen teenagers, stay-at-home moms, and frazzled couples. When they describe their daily lives, their relationships, and their actions, their stories all tend to be variations on the same theme: a pattern of behavior that repeatedly amps up the drama in their lives—patterns of behavior that lead to more *chaos*.

"Chaos" is defined by *Webster's Dictionary* as "any confused collection or state of things; complete disorder." Chaos-*addicted* individuals lack the ability to control the amount of disorder in their lives. They thrive on self-sabotage and destruction. Most often, it isn't simply that the chaos-addicted person is subject to bad luck. No, for them, bad things tend to happen so often because they go so far as to *manufacture* chaos-filled situations. Simply put, chaos addicts construct chaos-filled environments because it is exactly these environments to which they've grown accustomed. Chaos breeds chaos.

Chaotic behavior is hardly a new phenomenon. What *is* new are the factors in modern life that both contribute to and legitimize the behavior. More and more, we are pressured to further complicate our already complicated lives. And as we have begun to see over the years, complexity is rarely a good thing. Complexity tends to lead to a host of other problems: problems that take on many guises and forms, problems that only further exacerbate life's complexity. It is a vicious cycle—one that leads to equally vicious problems.

I have seen my share of chaos-addicted individuals and the consequences of leading such a lifestyle. I met plenty of them at Cal-Lutheran

College, where I received my undergraduate degree. The chaos only seemed to intensify in the lives of the students getting their masters in social work, who I shared my time with at UCLA. Certainly, my own life was chaotic and sometimes destructive as I crammed for test after test.

After garnering my masters, I have been working in private practice since 1990. I began my career in a residential treatment center for boys. Life then took me to the Capistrano by the Sea Hospital, where I spent seven years working with families and children on subjects such as anger management, anxiety, and depressive disorders. My private practice focus intensified in the two years I spent under the employment of the South Coast Medical Center, then became full-time when I branched out to start my own private practice.

But none of that qualifies me to write a book about chaos addiction quite as much as my own childhood does. Like so many people these days, my upbringing featured a great deal of stress. I was one among the many children in this country whose parents divorced. Unfortunately, however, the divorce didn't happen until well after my siblings and I were exposed to many years of turmoil and emotional mood-shifts.

See, my father was an alcoholic. And anyone who has ever known an addict understands the kind of chaos that alcoholism entails. Being the oldest child, it was my responsibility to shoulder the rollercoaster ups and downs of my father's mood swings. It was I who was left to console my mother whenever Dad got out of hand. Additionally, I bore the responsibility of explaining to my younger brother and sisters why these ugly situations and violent arguments always seemed to spring up between our parents.

But you don't need to be a habitual drinker or live with one to see how chaos can affect your own life and the lives of those around you. Many of us express our chaotic behavior in far subtler ways. The trouble with these subtle little expressions is that they tend to distress one's children, friends, and coworkers.

Like you, I eventually reached the point where I just didn't want to live this way anymore. Such was my desire to figure out why I always felt so stressed that I began digging beyond the typical symptoms and stressors that people look for. I began looking for solutions to the underlying problems instead of seeking quick fixes for the undesirable side effects.

I wish I could tell you that the solution I came across required thorough research and rigorous trial and error testing. But I can't. The truth is that it came to me on a lark. At the time, I was working with dual diagnosis patients—most of whom were suffering from some form of addiction, as well as depression. What I was seeing was patient after patient struggling with addiction, falling in line for the prescribed solutions of therapy, rehab, and sobriety, and then inevitably tumbling back into addiction. I witnessed the depression—the hopelessness—that comes along with living in such a cycle. And I saw it again and again.

It was then that I realized that there had to be something wrong with the picture of addiction therapy I had been given. There had to be a solution more effective than pushing the patients toward sobriety and sending them on their merry way. To me, the traditional rehab approach was like taking cold medication—it was like applying a drug to eliminate the *symptoms* rather than the *cause* of a cough or a runny nose. The short-term benefits might be desirable. The person who takes the cold meds can expect to enjoy twelve hours of normalcy. But the long-term problem goes unresolved. This same person might find himself taking cold meds for weeks on end. In fact, he might find that the act of taking the meds in the first place *prolongs* the cold.

There is more to therapy, more to self-improvement, than working on the symptoms. If any of us hopes to make change in our lives, we must focus not on the symptoms, but on the undercurrent of those symptoms. We must concentrate on eliminating the cause, rather than snuffing out the effect.

As mentioned, the method I've uncovered to address the cause of literally every iteration of chaos came to me almost on a whim. At the time, I was conducting a therapy group on balanced living. The people in the group were coming in to find solutions on how to make their lives a little less dramatic, stressful, and chaotic. I had come in to the session early, as always, so I could have some time to prepare the room and organize my thoughts. On this particular day, I was struggling with the feeling that I needed more structure for the talk I intended to give. I knew I was going to discuss the effects of chaos, where it comes from, and the varied reactions it tends to generate, but I didn't really have an outline or a model in mind. My chaos talk was looking just a little too chaotic.

And then it hit me. I should divide the notion of chaos into its four different stages. Then, I should assign each stage to an individual box. The chaos model that I would be left with would be cognitive and identifiable, simple and yet highly effective. So I took the chaos of everyday life, dissected the stressors that we all encounter on a daily basis, and fashioned them into their component parts. Further, I explained how to spot each stressor, each trigger of chaos, and how to cope with it in a more constructive way. I developed a simple alternative to the traditional methods of pushing medication and rehab—the traditional methods of applying fixes to the symptoms of a root cause rather than addressing the root cause itself.

When I presented the chaos model to my group that day, it was extremely well received. Everyone in the session loved it. They all embraced the concepts and went home with what they believed to be a viable alternative (or at least a workable supplement) to the failing solutions they had been exposed to time and time again over the years. But it was more than just hope. Those who were introduced to the chaos model began displaying remarkable signs of change. Addicts were remaining sober. Stressed parents were simplifying their routines. Depressed children were finding the joy in life once more.

So there was no scientific method to the development of this process. This is not to say that it hasn't generated verifiable results, however. Everyone I have introduced this method to has enjoyed remarkable change. Even those patients who have been into multiple rehabs have found success with the chaos model. Even parents who felt as if they were losing control have managed to establish new bonds with their kids. Even children whose lives were spiraling out of control have found solutions to turn things around.

Chaos *is* Addiction
Before we go any further, it's important to understand that alternate addictions may be little more than symptoms of a bigger problem: chaos addiction. Commonly diagnosed addictions such as alcoholism are developed as a result of one of the mind's most natural defense mechanisms: that of seeking a quick fix to a significant issue. We can treat the presenting addiction, but if we don't address the underlying force of the chaos addiction that underlies it, we're doing little more than applying a Band-Aid.

Dave is a forty-year-old who has frequently relapsed into alcoholism. He has been in rehab seven times, has gone to Alcoholics Anonymous, and has seen numerous therapists. Nothing seemed capable of stopping his addiction to alcohol—not even the threat of death. He had lost his marriage, as well as his right to see his children on a regular basis.

As Dave and I began to look at his life—his failure in jobs, relationships, and attempts to remain sober—we identified that his underlying issue was in fact an addiction to chaos. This addiction was derived from Dave's obsession with feeling important, being successful, and having financial security (the value of these characteristics had been drilled into him as a child, as his father was also an alcoholic, and had been extremely critical).

Whenever Dave was in rehab, he was treated for the alcoholism, but the undercurrents in his life were never addressed. For twelve years, Dave had been using alcohol as an excuse to feed his need for recklessness. Whenever he would get sober, he would have to face his insecurities. Obviously, this was uncomfortable for him. Sobriety would also mean boredom. He felt that calmness was boring and uncomfortable, and made him want to jump out of his skin.

Dave and I began to identify the triggers in his life and to see how his relapses were nothing more than reactions to these triggers. The problem was not the fact that he possessed these triggers; rather, the problem lay in his *reactions*. Most often, his reaction would be to seek more crisis and chaos. So we began to explore alternative potential decisions and reactions in the hopes that he could find more constructive ways to express himself in the face of problematic feelings. We determined wiser courses of action to take whenever Dave felt inadequate or frenzied. Instead of learning the ways to avoid alcohol, he learned how *not* to react to situations that he couldn't control, to focus on only those things that he had control over.

Dave developed an incredible decision tree that made him feel anchored and more secure. He began to see that the key to sobriety was not just giving up alcohol, but dealing with his fears. As he moved forward, it became important for him to experience periods of calmness and leisure and feel that it was okay to do so. He realized that, as a recovering chaos addict, it is more important to *feel* feelings and make wise decisions than to deny feelings and feed the chaos.

Dave is now two years sober and he no longer fears relapse. He works every day to simplify his life and make choices that will create balance. By doing something as simple as looking deeper into Dave's life and identifying his addiction to chaos—and applying methods and solutions to circumvent that chaos—we were able to break his cycle of alcoholism.

Modern Life Fuels Chaos

Fortunately for all of us, many things about our society have changed to make simple tasks far easier to complete. Unfortunately for all of us, these quick solutions have collectively led to a far more chaotic mode of existence. These days, most people feel they need to be doing twenty things at once just to feel productive. The rules have changed. Expectations have been raised and stress has increased exponentially.

Let's consider a few of the changes in modern society. New technology might support multi-tasking, but it's also made most of us far more impatient. And both conditions can be a prescription for chaotic choices. Fierce societal competition (to get into the right school, to get a better job, to be in the right club) creates a busyness that can detach us from thoughtful problem solving. Children whose daily lives are scheduled with the precision of a CEO's think that idleness is boring, so they become masters of drama and excitement—whirlwinds of negative energy. They come to believe that this busyness is directly related to their self-worth. The thrill becomes addictive; the cycle of chaos continues.

Consider the life of such a child. It shouldn't be difficult for you to imagine what it is like to be over stimulated, overbooked, and overscheduled. Almost all of us live our days exactly in this way. But for the child, such a lifestyle can be overwhelming. Whether this is owed to the fact that the parents' generation also grew up in largely chaotic environments is up for debate, but the fact remains that with each passing year, there seems to be more and more pressure to excel placed on children. Consider Advanced Placement classes, the push to graduate high school early (that way, they can graduate from college early), the drive to be in the top ten percent of a class in order to get into a good school, the increasing movement to put children through the rigors of extracurricular schoolwork and activities (learning a foreign language, taking music or dance lessons, participating in sports—both school affiliated and club affiliated—etc.). It seems that no matter where you live in this country, you will find children spending six hours at school only to be driven to soccer or baseball practice, followed closely by guitar lessons, followed by the demands of the Boy Scouts, followed by hours upon hours of homework (of which there seems to be an increasing amount each year). All of it adds up to little more than an overly hectic lifestyle. And a hectic lifestyle can only lead to increased opportunity for chaos and chaotic behavior.

Pressure to perform has trumped fun. Remember when sports used to be fun? Remember when social clubs used to be fun? Remember when high school used to be fun? Today, if it doesn't seem to the child like a burdensome obligation, then it's likely to seem to the child like an overly pressurized situation. Parents force their children to cram for exams, they urge them to participate in more and more activities, they scream from the stands. Even the activities that are supposed to be fun—sports, music lessons, social clubs—just aren't fun anymore.

Much has been made of the chaos that comes with today's media, as well. Take a child's life, with all this pressure to perform, and throw in violent, addictive, time-consuming, over-stimulating videogames, television, Internet media, music, and magazines, and what you have is a powder keg of chaos potential. Simple childhood imagination stands underutilized, simplistic play disappears (whatever happened to "Cops and Robbers"?), true fun goes ignored. Children have gotten to the point where they would rather wait up all night (on a school night, no less) and stand in line for fifteen hours outside their local electronics store all so they can pick up Halo 3 and spend the next three weeks glued to the television during every waking moment of free time. At ten years old, they stand in line with their parents at Starbucks every morning. They order their triple mocha latté and head to school. It is a dangerous cycle.

Add school itself to the mix. It's become a pressure-packed arena of social competition. There is more homework, more stress to fit in, and less opportunity to just be a kid. At home, little changes. The schedule is crammed. Sleep is sacrificed. Chaos runs amuck. And after all that, the child is sent back to school, where they have trouble paying attention, expressing themselves, even staying awake (that early afternoon three-espresso-shot crash can be devastating). For their trouble, they're misdiagnosed with autism or ADHD—and nobody bothers to ask them why they were staring out the window during arithmetic. There's no such thing as solving issues in this scenario, only diagnosing.

The Typical Chaotic Episode

Putting our children aside for a moment, a typical chaotic episode in our own lives might look like this: You choose to procrastinate with an important job project, knowing that the eleventh hour coincides with your wife's birthday party. That's the equivalent of taking a match to a gasoline-soaked pile of rags. At the dinner party, your cell phone keeps ringing because you're getting final project information. Your fire is now smoldering. Your wife is hurt because you have spoiled the dinner. So to make it up to her, you promise to take her to a movie the next day, knowing that you've promised to help a friend with his taxes. Now it's time to call the fire department!

Any of us can have moments, even periods, of chaotic behavior, but the true chaos addict puts one fire out, only to start another. Why do they do this? Because it feels good! Just as alcoholics use booze to quell their anxiety, chaos addicts use the adrenaline rush of drama to quell theirs. As we will see in later chapters, the cycle always starts with a trigger—a situation that taps into a subconscious feeling, such as fear, anger, or a sense of worthlessness. Rather than deal directly with the feeling, chaos addicts react impulsively, creating a negative diversion (over-scheduling, procrastinating, making a promise that can't be kept), which ramps up the adrenaline output. At some point, that impulsive reaction results in a "crisis" (missing an important appointment, messing up a critical presentation, angering a loved one), which kicks the chaos addict into "fight or flight" mode. The cycle ends when the addict either conquers the mess and feels like a hero ("See, I fixed it!") or flees the mess and denies responsibility ("It's not my fault!"). A period of calm will then set in but, make no mistake, it's only a prelude to the next act in the continuing saga.

Chaos addicts react impulsively to uncomfortable situations. Rather than stopping to think through how to deal with the possible conflict, they tend to do everything to increase the level of conflict—not deliberately, of course, but the result is the same.

So what is the payoff? Creating chaos that escalates into crisis pays several dividends. On an immediate level, it provides a diversion from unpleasant feelings such as anxiety, anger, jealously, or insecurity. It's also the ultimate boredom buster, even though the excitement it produces is ultimately stressful. It shields against intimacy, and it provides an easy self-definition. For high-functioning chaos addicts like Tom Marlin (who somehow clean up their own messes), it's validation that they really are okay. For low-functioning chaos addicts like Melissa Lowder (whose messes wreak havoc), it's proof that life is unfair. Either way, every time chaos addicts do fix a problem of their own making (nobody messes up *all* of the time), there's one more pay-off: They can delude themselves even longer that they might have life under control. Of course, they really don't!

We've come now to the end of this little introduction, and I have only one question for you: Does any of this (and I mean *any of this*) sound like you? If the answer is "yes," then you are sure to gain a great deal from the pages to come. Read on to discover how we all tend to breed chaos in our lives—and, more importantly, how we might all learn to overcome it.

Chapter 2

Defining Chaos

We live in a culture increasingly riddled by addictions of various types. Alcoholism, drugs, television, pornography, you name it and addictions to it are almost surely on the rise. But why? Did people in this country just suddenly become more prone to addiction, or is there something that lies deeper? I believe the latter.

It is important for us to reach the understanding that alternate addictions may in fact be a symptom of a much bigger problem: chaos addiction. Everyday addictions—the ones we hear so much about or maybe even battle ourselves—are not so much the root problem as they are the symptoms of that root problem. And just like with an illness of any kind, these symptoms should be viewed more like defense mechanisms. A person who works too often or too hard (the kind of person who has come to be called a workaholic) could well be using his job as a defense mechanism against a more significant life issue. An addiction to videogames—and their unique ability to let us unplug from the problems of everyday life—could be considered a defense mechanism. This is exactly why I refer to chaos addiction as "the mother of all addictions."

The Roots of Chaos

Chaotic behavior is generally learned in childhood, since children do not have the sophisticated defense mechanisms possessed by most adults. For most children, because stress is intangible, it tends to be a concept that they are not equipped to deal with. Their behavior is often reactionary and based entirely on the modeling of a parent or sibling. If the child's father is scattered, inconsistent and impulsive rather than deliberate, then the child will quite quickly come to embrace these same conditions. At times, a child's tendency toward chaotic behavior might instead be a reaction to outside stressors—a kind of coping mechanism. This is common in families in which one or more parent displays alcohol or rage problems. Conversely, the child may react unfavorably within a family with one or more parent who tends to be controlling or perfectionist in nature.

Regardless of the source of chaotic behavior, what is constant across the board is that chaos addiction tends to germinate in families in which problem-solving skills are limited and emotional issues are kept under wraps. The emotional avoidance can be overt: parents who simply squelch any display of feelings. It can be understandable: parents so distracted by a real crisis (a sick child, for example) that there's no room for other feelings. Or it can be subtle: well-meaning parents who are stretched so thin with work, children, and aging parents that there's simply no time on the schedule for emotional busyness.

When a child is stressed, we cannot be sure how he may be experiencing his world. While one sibling may respond to constant fighting between his parents by tuning it out, another may react to the same stress by fidgeting, squirming, and appearing distracted. Each child's behavior is an outlet for what he is feeling, and this behavior will eventually spill over into his social interactions.

Interestingly, we have seen a strange reaction from the environments in which children tend to operate most consistently. More and more, schools in this country are bypassing the potential for an underlying problem and automatically labeling children as suffering from Attention Deficit Disorder (ADD), Attention Deficit Hyperactive Disorder (ADHD), or even autism. If a child is easily distracted, disruptive in class, or not learning, he is slapped with one of these catch-all tags. The trouble with these convenient labels is that the vast majority of schools simply aren't looking deep enough to see the real problem.

According to a 2005 report by the Center for Disease Control, "prevalence estimates of ADHD in school-aged children have ranged from 2% to

18% in community samples." Imagine a community in which nearly one out of every five children is considered to be suffering from ADHD. If trends continue, this could become a reality in *every* community.[1]

According to a 2003 survey conducted by the National Survey of Children's Health, approximately 4.4 million children between the ages of four and seventeen had been reported diagnosed with ADHD. Of that 4.4 million, 2.5 million children were taking medication for the disorder. Two-and-a-half million children on drugs for a social disorder! And the worst part is that, in many cases, these drugs may not even be necessary as they are prescribed for the symptoms of a condition that society itself might very well be responsible for.[2]

Consider the following scenario:

Bobby has just come to school from a home where, at breakfast, his parents were yelling at each other and his dad hit his mom. Bobby witnessed this, and he was so upset that he couldn't even eat. Then, as he is rushed out the door, he is warned by his mother not to tell anyone what has happened. He arrives at school, very nearly late because of all that has happened.

When Bobby gets to class, he is (understandably) fidgety, keyed up, and unable to concentrate. He becomes disruptive and yells at the boy sitting next to him. Uh-oh! It's time for a trip to the school psychiatrist. Is Bobby really ADHD—as he will almost inevitably be labeled—or is his behavior a clue that something else might be going on in his life? This is the question that we need to be asking. Before labeling a child as ADD or ADHD, we should be assessing him for signs of chaos within his home or school environment. According to the CDC's 2005 Behavioral Risk Factor Surveillance System Survey, one in every four women in this country fall victim to domestic violence at some point during their lives. The same holds true for one of every nine men. And the numbers have steadily risen with each year.[3]

According to ChildHelp, a national hotline for child abuse claims, three million reports of child abuse claims are made in the U.S. every year. That amounts to one report of child abuse made every ten seconds. Four children die every day due to physical abuse in the home.[4]

These statistics are troubling enough on their own, but consider the fact that a child who grows up in this kind of atmosphere usually begins to initiate his own chaos, as well. Chaos is all he knows. He doesn't know what *calm* is, he doesn't know how to problem-solve, and he doesn't know how to make proper decisions. It's a learned behavior. He's copying the only thing that he knows. Unless you can teach a child to understand what he's feeling, break those same feelings down, put them in some form that he can understand and give him a few outlets through which to make decisions, he will continue to be a reactionary individual as he gets older. He will become angry at the drop of a hat. He will say and do things that he doesn't mean because that is all that he knows. It eventually becomes *who he is.*

I believe that there is a direct correlation between a child's family environment, and what he learns from it and produces on his own. For example, Nancy is a six-year-old whose divorced mother is extremely reactionary. The mother yells a lot, puts her daughter down, calls her names and generally demeans her at every opportunity. Mom has told the child that she never wanted her, that she wishes she didn't live with her, that she gets in the way of what the mother wants to do in life, and that she's the cause of her divorce. Unfortunately, Nancy now exhibits behavior that is similar to her mom's. She yells at other children, becomes overly aggressive, shows a lack of boundaries, puts others down and makes fun of them. In other words, she is modeling what is being taught to her by her mother.

These days, there are plenty of negative things to be learned from sources other than the parent. Videogames, television, and film have seen a tremendous increase in popularity amongst the youngest generation over the past decade. According to a survey conducted in 2007 by the Harris Poll, eight in ten young people in America report playing a videogame at least once per month. "The average 8- to 12-year-old now plays thirteen hours of video games per week." This might not be a problem if not for a few significant factors. Not only are videogames becoming more and more violent, but young gamers are experiencing terrible side effects as well. According to the Harris Poll, "8- to 18-year-olds who spend more time playing video games are more likely to" see a decline in school performance, get into fights, and gain weight.[5]

And according to the journal *Pediatrics*, the number of children exposed to graphic violence on television and film grows at an alarming rate. Today, more than twelve percent of children between the ages of ten to fourteen watch R-rated movies on a regular basis.[6]

The home is not the only environment where chaos is being modeled to children, either. I have touched on this subject briefly already—and it is debated endlessly in the media—but it still bears mentioning here. Children see chaos on television, at the movies, and in videogames every day. They hear it in their music. In modern pop culture, violence and fear-evoking situations run rampant. Superheroes are becoming more aggressive, their weapons more catastrophic. Videogames are bloodier and more realistic all the time. The killings depicted are progressively more violent. Children are being programmed, and I believe that we are seeing more incidents of violence because of this.

Because our society has become more reactive than proactive, chaos can be found everywhere. What do I mean by reactive? Take the following example: Schools claim that there is no money for preventive programs. They just don't have the funds. And yet, as soon as there is a shooting, a killing, or gang violence, funds suddenly become available for crisis counselors, extra security on campus, and metal detectors. We react to the crisis, but as soon as it subsides, we return to the old ways instead of continuing to look at ways to prevent the problem.

This, I believe, has a long-lasting effect on our children. They turn on the television and see shootings, not only in school, but also at the mall and in daycare centers. They feel unsafe wherever they go.

Ultimately, though, it is the parents' responsibility to provide a safe and calm atmosphere where a child can thrive, learn, and feel relaxed. If that child is growing up in an environment where the parents are constantly fighting and there is nothing but chaos in the home, there is no way he can remain calm or feel safe anywhere. It is almost as if he is in the middle of a war, and in order to survive, he has to become a part of that war. He can't stay separate because the parents will bring him into it anyway.

Divorce is becoming a greater concern, as well. Parents in the process of a divorce in which child custody is an issue often put their child in the middle by trying to force him to choose a side. They will use any tactic: vulgar language to make a point, guilt to get the child to take sides, and coaching the child on what to say. One parent will tell the child one thing while the other says something completely different: "You really should live with me, son, because your mother is a bitch." Or "If you don't live with me, I won't see you anymore." How can the child possibly know which parent to believe? And why must he be forced to believe one or the other in the first place?

All of this produces fear in the child. He feels that he must choose one parent and reject the other. He doesn't want to be put in this position because he usually loves both of his parents, but he's forced into it out of fear. With the divorce rate continuing to rise at an alarming rate, there is more and more of this happening.

In the end, children may adopt chaotic behavior as a coping mechanism because they are powerless to affect any real differences in their home or school lives. Such action eventually becomes an addictive habit—a habit that will require feeding well into adulthood.

What Chaos Addiction is *Not*

While much of the chaos model (and the anecdotes I use to highlight the finer points of the model) is rooted in the notion that people simply make their lives a little too busy these days, it is important to understand that not all busy people are chaos addicts. Not all chaos addicts are overbooked, overscheduled, and overloaded. Chaos addiction is also not to be confused with Attention Deficit Disorder (ADD) or Attention Deficit Hyperactivity Disorder (ADHD), nor is it general hyperactivity. Likewise, people genetically predisposed toward a more disorganized style of living (they thrive in clutter, keeping piles rather than files) are not necessarily chaos addicts unless they tend toward creating and escalating crises. The real sign of chaos addiction is a verifiable cycle of behavior that repeatedly creates personal or professional problems without ever working toward thoughtful resolution.

ADD is a neurobiological disorder affecting all aspects of a person's life. It causes the inability to focus, pay attention, and organize, as well as other symptoms. It may possibly be caused by an insufficiency of chemicals called neurotransmitters, which carry messages between brain cells. If these cells cannot communicate effectively, a person cannot organize and focus his intellectual resources.

Although there is no definitive test for ADD, preliminary studies reveal differences in brain chemical metabolism between those with ADD and those without. Because this disorder is a group of symptoms, diagnosis depends on the collection of data from various sources and settings. According to the *Iowa Health Book: Psychiatry*, diagnosing should include history and observations, norm-referenced behavior checklists, tests of intelligence and skills, and tests that rule out other possible conditions.

As I have touched on, a very possible reason that diagnosis for these disorders is on the rise is that they tend to mimic three different levels of stress: acute, episodic acute, and chronic stress.

Acute stress is the most common form. It comes from demands and pressures of the recent past and anticipated demands and pressures of the near future. For example, a child who has just witnessed verbal or physical violence in the home may not be able to relax enough to focus academically when he gets to school. He may have trouble staying seated, lose or forget things, shift from one unfinished task to another, interrupt, not wait his turn, blurt out answers before a question is finished, even complain that normal activities are boring. These behaviors may be consistent, but are certainly not limited, to an ADD child.

Episodic acute stress results when a person experiences intermittent chaos. Symptoms may include overstimulation, a short temper, irritability, and feelings of anxiety (also known as "nervous energy"). Episodic stress may come from ceaseless worry. The person may view the world as dangerous and unrewarding because he is always anticipating the next negative event in his life.

Finally, chronic stress is grinding, wearing a person down day after day, year after year. The person may reach the point where he cannot see any way out of a miserable situation. He often feels that he has no means of controlling, changing, or leaving a given situation. Children are just as vulnerable to chronic stress as adults are, even though they may be unable to vocalize these feelings.

Because of the similarities between ADD and stress, it is important that a person take a good look at his life to assess the amount of chaos and the possibility of an addiction to said chaos.

As I mentioned, not all busy people can be called chaos addicts. Not all busyness can be construed as a symptom of chaotic behavior. When taking a look at your own hectic life to determine whether you have a chaos problem, there are a few important points to consider.

First, there is one key difference between people who maintain a healthy profile of busyness and people who find themselves locked in a constant chaos cycle. We cannot simply take a look at your calendar and see that you have a full plate—work out in the morning, go to work (and take on a schedule packed with meetings and client calls), pick up the kids, drop the kids off at practice, cook dinner, go to card club, etc.—and automatically bill you a chaos addict. Believe it or not, it is possible to be busy and still remain balanced.

Here's the difference: Busy and yet balanced people *schedule their time reasonably*. They may have a workout followed by work followed by a full evening of personal activities, but if they schedule time for their daughter's softball game, they *actually have time* to watch their daughter's softball game.

What do I mean by that? For the answer, let's take a look at the contrast point: the chaos addict. Someone locked in a chaos cycle has a busy schedule, yes. The only problem is that their schedules are consistently *over*booked. In the case of the chaos addict, the daughter's softball game is scheduled for 4:15 p.m. (and he promises to attend), only he never makes it because he booked an important client call for four o'clock on the same day. The worst part is that he doesn't tend to see the problem with this situation until it's too late. Instead of realizing that he will never make his daughter's game this way, he stretches himself too thin, attempts to be in two places at once, and is stressed to no end because of it. Incidentally, having to apologize to his daughter afterwards tends to lead to even more stress.

The chaos addict always over schedules. He's always talking about how he needs to get down to the gym, but then never goes (there's just no time). He's constantly late for important personal or even professional engagements (he had other things on the schedule that he needed to wrap up first). He's always skipping lunch (there's just so much to get done). He's constantly complaining that there isn't enough time in the day to do everything he needs to do. He's constantly apologizing for his inability to properly manage time.

So there's the primary difference. Someone who is busy in a healthy way can handle his own schedule. Someone who is busy in an unhealthy way tends to lead the life of the chaos addict. This latter person chooses to over schedule, assuming that he will be able to make things work out once the scheduled time arrives. He'll cross that bridge when he comes to it, as if he will magically figure out a way to be in two places at once.

The good news is that it doesn't have to be this way. Some people have busy lives, but they still manage to maintain balance. They *schedule* time to have lunch, go to the gym, see their daughter's softball game. There *is* enough time in the day to do all that you need to do. And you don't need better time management skills. All you need is to take control. Remember, choosing to be overly busy is still a choice. Slotting three things into one hour on your schedule is still a choice—and a poor one, at that. You *can* take control of your chaotic lifestyle. You *do* have the ability to be on time, have time, make time. Your job is not to blame. Your other personal or professional commitments are not to blame. The problem lies within.

Chaos Addiction: Anyone Can Fall Victim

No one personality type is most susceptible to becoming addicted to chaos. The addict can be any age, any gender, make a lot of money or very little money, and be overly busy or not busy at all. What these people share is a variety of characteristics that contribute to the constant production of chaos. They can be positive, negative, and truly destructive.

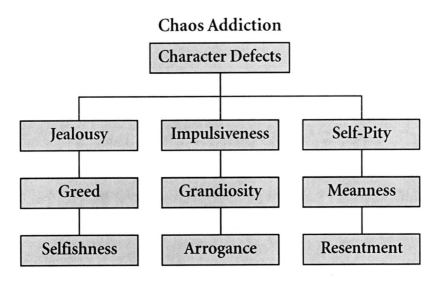

On the positive side, chaos addicts can be generous, spontaneous, humorous, creative and helpful—but always in a way that creates another crisis (think of Melissa Lowder from Chapter 1; she was always helping a co-worker at the expense of her own productivity). On the negative side, a chaos addict may be impulsive, forgetful, consistently tardy, and counterproductive. Truly destructive chaos addicts will lie, deny, finger-point, display arrogance, and harbor feelings of grandiosity.

The level of chaos addiction may vary, as well. Let's separate the chaos addict into two classes: high-functioning and low-functioning. A high-functioning chaos addict may be considered successful professionally and personally. Low-functioning chaos addicts can be prone to multiple job changes and relationship problems. But regardless, for each, under the crisis-riddled surface, one will almost always find a layer of anxiety, loneliness, anger, self-pity, grief, or resentment; it just varies by degree.

So how do you know if you are addicted to chaos? You may be addicted if:

- You find yourself incapable of avoiding negative situations even though you may want to. In other words, every time you get past one chaotic situation, you seem to find yourself mired in another. If chaos is so frequent in your life, it is most likely because you have a tendency to *create* it.
- You realize that you are suffering from other addictions to things such as drugs, alcohol, sex, gambling, or food.
- You tend to start arguments or fights deliberately.
- You occasionally avoid returning home when you said you would—even if your original plan was to actually return home on time.
- You act foolish or alter your personality when you become uncomfortable in a situation.
- You refuse to admit that your life is unmanageable. You make up excuses to justify your behavior ("This is who I am and there is nothing wrong with me").
- You feel the need to partake in dangerous or illegal activities.
- You repeat the same patterns of behavior (wondering all the time why you always end up with the same outcome).
- Your spiritual beliefs become less important as you try to justify your actions and make excuses for your mistakes.

For the chaos-addicted individual, life is like living in a self-imposed jail (and a particularly hellish one, at that). There is no balance and the cycle seems inescapable. And in the end, the worst part is the fact that creating chaos actually takes more time, energy, money, and love than creating balance, but the addict doesn't realize this.

More Symptoms of Chaos Addiction

In my time studying the cycle of chaotic behavior, I have uncovered a series of specific symptoms that can be attributed to the chaos addict, however severe the case. For the purpose of clarity, I will list the symptoms first, then move on to define each of them.

Symptoms of Chaos Addiction
- Personalizing
- Magnifying
- Minimizing

- Either/or thinking
- Thinking out of context
- Jumping to conclusions
- Over-generalizing
- Self-blame
- Magical thinking
- Mind reading
- Comparing
- Catastrophe thinking
- Negativity

Now, let's take a closer look at each of these symptoms and see if we can get to the bottom of their meaning.

Personalizing
This symptom refers to the tendency of the chaos addict to think that all situations and events revolve around him. Whatever negative situation is playing out, the addict believes that he is the center of it, even when he is clearly not. "Everyone was looking at me and wondering why I was there."

Magnifying
This symptom refers to the tendency of the chaos addict to blow negative events way out of proportion. Whatever negative situation arises, in the addict's mind, its significance is magnified well beyond reality. "This is the worst thing that has ever happened to me."

Minimizing
This symptom refers to the tendency of the chaos addict to gloss over the positive factors of a given situation. The addict tends to fixate on the negative in every occurrence, greatly minimizing whatever positives may come up. To a certain degree, minimizing is akin to denial.

Either/Or Thinking
This symptom refers to the tendency of the chaos addict to ignore the gray area in most situations. In other words, the addict often fails to take the full picture into account. Either they consider themselves to be (or consider the situations they find themselves getting into) one extreme or another. "Either you're a winner or you're a loser."

Thinking out of Context
This symptom is similar to magnifying and minimizing, only it refers to specific events. Thinking out of context is the tendency of the addict to fixate on the negative portion of a given event. For example, after a successful job interview, the addict will tend to focus on his performance during one or two tough questions. "I blew the whole interview" or "I completely bombed that exam."

Jumping to Conclusions
This symptom is also similar to magnifying and minimizing, only this refers to a tendency toward melodrama. The chaos addict tends to take the smallest warning signs and maximize them to the point of absurdity. "I have a swollen gland. This must be cancer."

Over-Generalizing
This symptom refers to the tendency of the chaos addict to take a small cross-section of his life and use it as the complete definition of his self-worth. "I always fail" or "I fail at everything I try."

Self-Blame
This symptom refers to the tendency of the chaos addict to shoulder blame for everything. Even with negative events that can be attributed to multiple people, the addict assumes absolute fault. "I'm no good" or "It's all my fault."

Magical Thinking
This symptom refers to the tendency of the chaos addict to assume that his chaotic lifestyle can be attributed to some higher force. This is the direct result of his desire to avoid taking control of or responsibility for his own actions. "Everything is bad for me because of the things I've done in my past."

Mind Reading
Similar to personalizing, this symptom refers to the tendency of the chaos addict to assume that everyone around him is thinking negatively about him. Regardless of what people might be thinking, the addict always assumes it is destructive or insulting. "Everyone thought I was fat and ugly."

Comparing

This symptom refers to the tendency of the chaos addict to compare himself to others. These comparisons are almost constant—and usually weight unfavorably against the addict. "He's so much smarter than me."

Catastrophe Thinking

This symptom refers to the tendency of the chaos addict to assume the worst in a given event. Regardless of the favorability of the situation in question, the addict will project the worst possible scenario. "I know something terrible is going to happen" or "This whole thing is going to be a disaster."

Negativity

Obviously, this final symptom underlies all other symptoms listed above. It is important to note that anyone can be negative. Also, anyone can occasionally be susceptible to the symptoms listed above. What separates the negativity of the chaos addict from healthy negativity is that, for the chaos addict, the negativity is nearly constant. The default assumption is always negative.

The Damaging Effects of Chaos Addiction

Left unchecked, chaos addiction can lead to physical, emotional, and spiritual problems of all sorts. The chaos of an addict's schedule eventually bleeds into all aspects of his lifestyle. Let's take a look at just a few of the consequences.

Physical Consequences
- Insomnia
- Irregular eating habits
- Illness
- Loss of interest in personal appearance
- Decline in personal hygiene
- Decline in sexual desire

Intrapersonal Consequences
- Feelings of guilt and shame
- Loss of interest in activities previously enjoyed
- Moral and spiritual degradation (including confusion between right and wrong)

- An increase in the tendency toward trouble (owed mostly to a trend toward reactionary behavior)
- Loss of personal growth or sense of purpose

Interpersonal Consequences
- Family and friends notice a change in behavior
- Alienation of family members
- Harsher and crueler behavior
- Strains form within the marriage
- Old friendships are lost
- New friendships tend to be unhealthy

Social Responsibility Consequences
- Increased frequency of missing school or work
- Degradation of the quality of work
- Balancing money and finances becomes more difficult or begins to seem less important

Impulse Control Consequences
- Increased tendency to become involved with drugs, alcohol, gambling, or sex
- Tendency toward binge eating
- Rise in risk taking or foolish/impulsive behavior
- Spike in the tendency toward regret
- Increase in physical violence
- Increase in illegal behavior
- Increase in reactionary behavior

Unfortunately, in the society in which we now live, we tend to view these symptoms and consequences as problems themselves rather than signs of something more significant. We still treat symptoms instead of central problems. We treat the drug and alcohol abusers, we counsel the violent and manic, we offer "time management solutions" for the overscheduled, but we don't address the underlying problems that cause such behavior. We can treat these presenting symptoms—we can offer rehab or methadone for the addict—but if we don't deal with the chaos at the center of it all, relapse will surely recur. The chaos addict will inevitably find another addiction to camouflage what he's really feeling underneath.

So it is time that we take hold of this problem and work toward a common solution. Read on to discover a model for chaotic behavior that will help you to identify sources of stress and chaos in your own life. Once we have identified the sources, we can work toward improving your quality of life and breaking the cycle of chaos.

Chapter 3

The Chaos Model

During my time in practice, I have observed the viciousness of the chaos cycle time and time again. My observations have led to the development of what I have dubbed the Chaos Model, a visual representation of the choices all of us make in our lives on a regular basis. The model itself, divided into four quadrants (or boxes), has been used by a great many of my clients to help them re-envision appropriate responses to chaos and other stressors. Regardless of where they have stood on the chaos spectrum, all have seen tremendous results with this model.

Before we get into the nuts and bolts of the model itself, however, it would be prudent to examine a group of people who have enjoyed such results. Now, as always, I have changed the names to protect the innocent, but the stories of the following family of four certainly ring true. From the very beginning, they were clear candidates for the Chaos Model—and these days, thanks to the model, they are seeing remarkable improvement in the quality of their lives.

The Dawsons
Without further ado, let's introduce John Dawson. John, forty-three, considers himself the head of his family of four. Being the sole bread-

winner, he often feels justified in demanding an unreasonable amount of support from his wife, Julie, a forty-year-old stay-at-home mother. The stress of his job often leaves him exhausted and exasperated by the time he gets home—and, unfortunately for his wife and two children, this tends to lead to a fair deal of yelling.

Early on in the marriage, John's yelling seemed almost rational to Julie. He would only yell when the situation called for it—say one of his children broke the antique lamp in the living room, for example. But more and more, John has begun yelling about everything: about clutter around the house, about getting cut off in traffic on the way home, about Julie leaving him with an empty tank of gas, about the unruly barking dog that greets him at the door, about a bad call by the referee penalizing his favorite football team. It all adds up. For a while, it had begun to seem like John had forgotten what it was like to speak at a normal volume. He was a walking terror of screaming and complaining.

Julie's life has changed pretty dramatically in seventeen years of marriage, as well. Even though it was an unplanned pregnancy that caused her to marry John at an age when she didn't feel ready, she has always loved him. Lately, however, she finds herself resenting him. Not because of his yelling—the yelling she can bear, so long as it doesn't continue to build at the rate it has over the past few years—but because of John's job. From the very beginning, she agreed that it would be best for her to stay home and care for Jenny, their eldest child. And she does not regret this decision in any way. She simply didn't expect to have to work as a stay-at-home mom for the rest of her life. But when Jimmy came along, the decision was made that she would continue to stay home.

Julie reacted to what she is increasingly considering a shortfall in her life by doing a couple of things. First, she overbooked herself and her children to the point of ridiculousness. She has so many obligations that she does not have time to do what most stay-at-home moms are asked to do—which, of course, puts further stress on Julie and further strain on the marriage. What's worse, her relationship with her children is degrading because she finds herself feeling like less the mother and more like the slave-driver. And second, she has begun to resent John more and more for his career. Obviously, something has to give.

Jenny, the eldest of the two children at seventeen years old, has done what most seventeen-year-olds do: She has begun to rebel against her parents. Her rebellion began at fifteen, right around the time when her schedule became more than she could bear. Between expectations at school, expectations with the volleyball/basketball/softball team, expectations of her music teacher and dance instructor, and expectations of her doting mother and father, something has *already* broken down for Jenny.

Slowly, Jenny began giving up things that had previously brought her joy. She quit dancing and playing the flute. She quit the basketball team. Her grades began slipping. All because she never felt as if she had any time to herself. At sixteen, she began experimenting with drugs. By now, the experiment has turned the corner toward a full-on addiction. Unless she can sort out a way to manage the chaos in her life, Jenny is headed for serious trouble at a very young age.

Jimmy is the baby of the family and has always been treated as such. But at nine years old, he has just entered the stage in his life when being babied does not seem so wonderful anymore. He wants to feel responsible now. Unfortunately, this is not the natural mindset of a nine-year-old. Jimmy has most likely gotten to this point thanks to years of unnaturally heavy workloads. Just like Jenny, he is expected to perform in school, complete his homework efficiently, and attend any number of social and athletic activities. He has taken to this fact rather differently than Jenny, however. While his sister uses drugs, Jimmy uses his free time to plug in to his videogames, his iPod, his computer—anything to separate him from his by-the-minute world.

What's more, Jimmy is at an age when watching his parents argue is a far more impressionable event. While Jenny can maybe cope with the frequent spats between her parents (though the way she copes is destructive), Jimmy has no coping mechanism. His parents' strain becomes strain on himself and his own life. And all the while he is learning that a dispute is best solved with yelling, with irrational argument. The seeds of chaos are being laid most deeply in Jimmy. Unless something is done to turn things around, his chaos addiction will spiral out of control before he even has a chance.

Balance vs. Chaos

Remember Tom Marlin? He's always misplacing things. This may trigger feelings of frustration and anxiety when he is under a time crunch to find them. His reactions cause chaos for not only him but also his wife and secretary. Maybe it's his car keys that he is always losing. If Tom would make the decision to put his keys in the same place every time he lays them down at home or in his office, then the chaos of frantically looking for them would disappear.

Nancy Garson is always paying exorbitant phone bills and service charges. This triggers feelings of anger with the bank or the phone company. She blames them instead of herself. A good decision would be to make a list of the things she will need for her weekend trip, then check off each item as she completes it.

It is little solutions like these that make all the difference. Later on in the book, you will be offered tips and strategies to help you avoid your most commonly chaotic situations. And as you will see, the best and only way to do this is to seek out solutions that will bring more balance into your life. See, balance is the antithesis of chaos—It is its most direct opposite. With steadfast focus on the strategies that you will carefully construct, your path to balance will steadily become clearer than your path to chaos.

The following graphic serves as a mere introduction to the concept of chaos versus balance. It should give you an idea as to what a 'balance' decision looks like when compared to a 'chaos' decision. The goal of this book is not only to get you thinking about balance decisions such as the ones that follow, but to provide you with solutions as to how to incorporate them into your everyday life, as well.

Chaos vs. Balance

CHAOS		BALANCE	
✗	Finger Pointing	✓	Discussion
✗	Intimidation	✓	Time Out
✗	Lying	✓	Grain of Salt
✗	Irresponsibility	✓	Kindness
✗	Violence	✓	Compassion
✗	Denial	✓	The Other View
✗	Accusation	✓	Humility

Facing the Chaos Cycle and Identifying the Triggers

At the start of this chapter, I outlined four stories of people who encounter chaos rather frequently. And I have done this for a reason: In the chapters to come, each of the four sample victims of the chaos cycle will be walked through one individual box of the Chaos Model. Through their stories, light will be shed on appropriate and inappropriate responses to daily stressors, as well as a few actions you can take to help avoid the possibility of chaos gaining control over your life.

Maybe there are a few points in each illustration above that you find yourself identifying with directly, but for the purposes of outlining the Chaos Model as a whole, let's take a look through a lens that we can all identify with: childhood. As I have already mentioned, these days, the cycle of chaos begins pretty forcefully at childhood, so it represents the perfect springboard for the model.

The Chaos Model

Box 1: **Triggers/Feelings**	**Box 2:** **Decisions**
Box 3: **Reactions**	**Box 4:** **Chaos**

In this chapter and the chapters to come, we will examine the model above in a left to right, top to bottom format. So first, let's take a look at the upper left box, the one labeled "Triggers/Feelings." Of the four boxes, you will notice that this is the only one that carries a two-word name. This is for good reason. The notion of feelings—the way we feel in reaction to a particular stimulus—works hand in hand with the stimulus itself (or the trigger). In other words, you can't have a feeling without something that triggers that feeling.

But let's take this idea one step further. Triggers, as I have defined them, often produce constructive or even desirable feelings, but they also often produce unwanted feelings. It is this latter category of feelings that needs to be slowed if we hope to make any progress. Unless negative feelings are examined thoroughly, we cannot properly assess their triggers, which is the first step toward preventing the ensuing chaos that may occur.

So let's talk about this in terms of a child. Jimmy Dawson, as mentioned, is nine years old, and just like most of us, when he experiences a feeling, it is always related to some sort of trigger.

Now, Jimmy doesn't think of his daily emotional fluctuations in terms of their corresponding triggers, but that doesn't mean that the triggers aren't significant. Jimmy knows that he dreads going down to the bus stop before school. He dreads it so much, in fact, that his mother, Julie, has difficulty getting him out the door each morning. This, of course, troubles his mother, as she can't figure out why a boy who loves school so much (as Jimmy certainly does) would hate getting ready and heading off to it.

It isn't distaste for school that makes Jimmy struggle against Mom and then walk slowly to the bus stop. It isn't that buses are often loud and uncomfortable that makes him wish he could just stay in bed. And it most definitely isn't that Jimmy doesn't like to learn or play with his friends. What keeps Jimmy from wanting to stand at the bus stop? Fear. Anger. Anxiety.

And what triggers these feelings? The neighborhood bully, of course. Steven, we will call him. Lately, Steven has begun to pick on Jimmy on a regular basis, making fun of him and calling him names. Soon, Jimmy fears, he will begin to move from the emotional to the physical torment. Steven has threatened as much, anyway.

So that, in a nutshell, is the significance of the Triggers/Feelings box. We will get into it in more detail in Chapter 4, but for now, understand that Triggers/Feelings is the catalyst—exterior forces and interior feelings working in tandem to set the whole chaos cycle in motion. Without a thorough working knowledge of this box and what it means within our own lives, we cannot hope to work through the Chaos Model and rid our lives of chaos once and for all.

If the first box in the Chaos Model represents the situations we are presented with and the way we feel when we encounter them, then the natural next step would be the decisions we make regarding these situations and feelings. In this way, the "Decisions" box is perhaps the most critical of the four. For most chaos-addicted individuals, this quadrant of the model is often mismanaged or underutilized.

Say that Jimmy has arrived at the bus stop this morning. He sees three of his friends shifting from side to side, talking, laughing, and waiting for the bus. A few of the girls in his class skip up the sidewalk ahead of him and file in to greet the others in the group. Predictably, Steven is also there—and he seems to be waiting only for Jimmy. His vindictive eyes train on him as he approaches.

Jimmy gulps and shuffles up to the bus stop. He is so anxious already that he doesn't even say hello to his friends. He keeps his head down and his shoulders scrunched up, maybe in the hopes of not being seen by the bully standing not six feet away. Just as his friends greet him, Steven begins his latest routine. He teases Jimmy mercilessly.

Jimmy's friends go red in the face and bury their hands in their pockets, looking away from Steven. One of the girls laughs, the other politely asks Steven to stop making fun of people. The bully does not listen. He simply continues pestering poor Jimmy.

As our Chaos Model suggests, Jimmy now has a decision to make. This decision, in turn, can be divided into two groups. Either Jimmy will react immediately—certainly a rash decision that will lead to chaos—or he can stop to think about what might be the best course of action to take—a calculated decision that might bring more balance to his morning.

So if Jimmy chooses to react, he might find himself calling his bully names or even picking a fight. But if Jimmy takes the time to think before he reacts, then he might just do exactly what his mother has always told him to do: just walk away. This will remove the chaos from the situation.

Now if this all seems fairly straightforward, that is a good thing. This model is not intended to be complicated or confusing. But with that said, let's cover the other arm of the decision process.

"Reaction" is the box that leads to so many problems for so many people addicted to chaos. People who grew up with chaos in their lives—or otherwise find themselves locked in a cycle of chaotic behavior—most often tend to skip the "Decision" box and go straight from "Triggers/Feelings" to "Reaction." In other words, people who live heavily in the Reaction box do not tend to "stop and think." They simply let their lives become overrun with knee-jerk and emotionally-driven reactions. More often than not, reactions are not rational, to say nothing of beneficial to the balance in one's life. So relying upon them (whether consciously or subconsciously) can lead to any number of chaos-driven problems.

As I already mentioned, in the case of Jimmy, the natural reaction would be to do and say things that he does not mean. If he reacts to his triggers/feelings instead of taking the time to decide upon the best course of action, he is most likely to wind up in a fistfight.

This brings us conveniently to our fourth box: "Chaos." By now you should recognize the sources of (or at least the potential for) chaos in your life. It is the source of stress and negative behavior that we all are sometimes (or often) subjected to.

If Jimmy bypasses his problem-solving skills and delves straight into his Reaction box, chaos will come into play. Jimmy and the bully will get into a fight. Jimmy, being a formidable fighter despite his diminutive size, will wind up giving Steven a black eye. Jimmy, also being a boy with a sensitive heart, will feel upset for having hurt the bully: chaos. Steven will surely run home and tell his parents, which will get Jimmy into trouble with his own parents: chaos. The school will also find out about the altercation, leading to a suspension for Jimmy: chaos. Jimmy's absence will cause him to fall behind in school, dropping his grades in the process: chaos.

You see how all of this can snowball and spiral out of control.

As a quick recap, here is the entire negative process: Chaos begins with the first box, "Triggers/Feelings." This produces feelings of anger, anxiety, or fear, which results in the bypassing of the "Decision" box in favor of "Reaction," the *third* box. Good problem-solving techniques are foregone to make way for the less favorable reaction. In the end, more chaos is created.

The problem with this negative path through the model is that it is the most common. Jimmy is quicker to bend toward reaction rather than decision because he has seen this behavior so often at home: fighting parents, a yelling match over his homework, anxiety about the local news, etc. Further, Jimmy has seen on television and played in any number of videogames scenarios exactly like the one he has found himself in on this day. The fight response has literally become a learned behavior. This is all that he knows, and he has become conditioned to it.

What other reactions, what other forms of chaos, can we condition ourselves to? This is exactly the question that the four chapters to come intend to answer.

So you see the underlying point of the Chaos Model: to get people to trend toward the positive path—to help people like Jimmy think first before reacting to feelings. But before we can do that, we must first come to terms with where we stand as people who confront chaos on a daily basis. The central question is this: "Do I have control over everything that happens to me every day?"

The simple answer is, of course, "No." It is not possible for you to control every aspect of your life, every occurrence that you encounter. But it is possible to control *some* things. And the most important of these things is how you respond to your triggers/feelings. Are you a decider or a reactor?

For Jimmy, he must learn that it is up to him to decide the best solution to reducing the triggers set in motion by his bully, Steven. If he can do this, he can avoid vaulting into the "Reaction" box in a negative way.

This isn't just for Jimmy, either. It isn't just children who can rewrite their most common responses to triggers/feelings. In fact, this same model can be applied to adults who have developed lifelong patterns of chaos. It can be employed to help you overcome even your deepest of chaos addictions.

Chapter 4

Box 1: Triggers/Feelings

So now that we have the nuts and bolts of the Chaos Model down, we can begin to build upon the foundation and go into greater detail on each of the four boxes. As the title of this chapter suggests, we will begin with "Triggers/Feelings"—the catalyst of the Chaos Model and the hinge point of the great internal balance versus chaos debate.

If you recall, Box 1 of the Chaos Model is a dual threat of sorts. Understanding its wiles is also the core of everything we, as individuals influenced by chaos, hope to achieve. The word "Triggers" refers to everything in our life that might spark a feeling of any kind. It is the stimuli that surround us at every moment of every day. A trigger itself can be broken down into two groups, as well. Either you have a positive trigger (a stimulus with the potential to seed a positive reaction such as laughter or joy) or a negative trigger (a stimulus with the potential to seed a negative reaction such as yelling or anger). For most people, the positive triggers in life stand in balance with the negative triggers—they often put themselves in a position to see a range and variety of triggers on a given day. For some, the positive triggers far outweigh the negative triggers—certainly an enviable position to be in. And for many, the negative triggers rule the day. For this last type of person, chaos is an easy addiction to succumb to.

The other half of Box 1 is equally significant—some would say more so, since it represents the first point where the struggle against chaos becomes truly internal. A trigger exists outside the body. If one finds oneself in a situation riddled with negative triggers, one can simply avoid that situation in the future, after all. But, of course, that's overly simplistic. Not all situations can be avoided. The negative trigger-ridden situation could be one's job or one's home life, for example.

Given all that, the way we *feel* about triggers, whether positive or negative, becomes incredibly important to understand. If we can get a handle on how we feel about the things that set us off, we can begin to make verifiable predictions about future behavior, which in turn makes the task of moving toward balance and away from chaos all the more manageable.

So we have now reached an understanding of the significance of Box 1. Triggers instantaneously breed feelings within us. Those feelings will either lead us toward a decision or a reaction, which in turn leads to balance or chaos, respectively. But to shed better light on this subject, let's examine a trigger-rich situation that almost all of us can identify with: the "joy" of sitting in rush hour traffic.

Gridlock: Chaos' Playground

On a typical day, John Dawson is a fan of leaving work around 4:30 p.m. It's not that he's a lazy employee—he has been in the office since seven-thirty this morning, after all. It's just that he knows that if he doesn't leave at four-thirty, it will take him a full ninety minutes to get home. John understands that rush hour traffic holds the potential for a great many negative triggers—and as a result, a slew of bad feelings—and has attempted to reconstruct his day in the hopes of avoiding the issue.

But you see the problem with avoiding the issue. For one thing, John must wake up far earlier than he normally would just to make up for lost time at work. This puts pressure on him to get more done for his family before leaving at 6:30 a.m. It also essentially keeps him under the thumb all day, as he feels compelled to check the clock every hour, just to make sure he isn't running late and can leave at his chosen time.

So John already understands the overarching trigger that is represented by rush hour traffic, and arriving early and leaving early from work is his chaos-fueled reaction. This is John's flawed coping mechanism.

On this day, John is unfortunately running late. As a draftsman, he often works under tight deadlines, and this day is no different. He had been tied up on a client call in the early afternoon, which of course put him behind on his day's busywork. Unfortunately, he knows that he cannot leave the office until his drafts are in. So he must stay a half hour later than he would have liked, placing him squarely in the rush hour danger zone of five o'clock.

In fact, when John finally does tear himself away from his desk, by the time he's turned in his work, said his goodbyes, found his car in the company's vast parking lot, and sat down in the driver's seat, his dashboard clock reads 5:03. He knows he's in trouble. With a groan, he starts the car. With a whimper, he pulls out of the parking lot. And feeling very sorry for himself, he merges into gridlock.

Swirling all around him are literally thousands of triggers. Each potential move that can be taken by each car in John's immediate vicinity bears the possibility of seeding a negative feeling in John. The giant, rumbling, heavily polluting, full-sized truck to his left provides the bass for the soundtrack of evening traffic. All around, at varying distances, the horns take up their unruly symphony. From time to time, John knows that he will lean on his own horn, but not now. Not yet.

Just ahead, he sees that he has the good fortune of following the "unpredictable braker." This is the kind of person whose brake lights seem to flash on and off for no apparent reason. They brake too early. They drive too quickly. They come to a halt just in the nick of time, forcing John to do the same. Just ahead of the rumbling truck is an oversized SUV driven by a middle-aged man not so different from John. The only difference is that this middle-aged man seems to think it acceptable to eat during rush hour. His concentration on his food causes him to make a number of wild and erratic moves within traffic, and he appears in grave danger of causing a wreck.

To John's right, merging from the latest in an endless array of on-ramps, is a luxury sedan piloted by a young woman talking on her cell phone. She merges slowly and tactlessly, not doing anything to let John know her intentions. Just ahead of her is a long, boat-like Buick piloted by a very old man. He seems to have his wife beside him. And he definitely doesn't realize that he has his right turn signal on. It will flash arbitrarily for many miles.

Behind John is the real kicker. He sees this woman only in his rearview, but he gets enough of a sense of her to know that this will be a long journey home. Every thirty seconds or so, she furrows her brow, scowls, and absolutely lays on her horn. She does this so often that John begins to think that she actually believes honking will spur traffic onward.

So here is John Dawson: literally stuck in a vast sea of negative triggers. The feelings it breeds in him? Understandably negative.

John Dawson: Road Rage Addict

Now that we have set the scene and laid out all the triggers, let's take a look at what John's commute might look like if he reacts to the negative feelings he receives from those triggers.

Having just cleared a bottleneck, traffic seems to be picking up slightly. The great wave of cars revs up its collective engine and surges forward, creating separation between John and the unpredictable braker ahead of him. The unpredictable braker overestimates the gap between him and the car in front of him, however, and when traffic inevitably slows back to a crawl, he is forced to slam on his brakes.

John, fiddling with the volume dial on his radio (it's just too loud outside the car to hear anything within it, so he has to crank it up to near the maximum level), sees the brake lights ahead of him at the last possible moment. He slams his foot down, bringing his car to a stop mere centimeters from the bumper ahead of him. His heart races. His blood pressure roils. His anger seethes. He shakes his head in frustration, grinding his sweaty palms back and forth over the wheel.

As is the case with any traffic pattern, if you don't like the pace, just wait five seconds; it will change. After only a moment or two of standstill— which John spends by fuming and fussing—the unpredictable braker takes off, creating a small gap between him and John. The young woman on her cell phone uses the opportunity to cut into John's lane, nearly clipping his hood. Furious now, John mashes his hand on the horn, glowering at the young woman, hoping desperately that she will see him in her rearview. Of course she will not, as she continues to chat away on her cell phone.

John looks to his left and to his right (he finds himself in the center lane of a five-lane highway now) and realizes that, as far as pace is concerned, he has picked the worst possible lane in which to travel. His lane moves most slowly—a speed matched only by the lane directly to his right. It isn't long before he realizes why. The elderly couple in the Buick, right turn signal still blaring, seems to be swerving arbitrarily back and forth between the two slow-moving lanes.

His skin practically crawling with frustration, John decides that it is time to merge left—only, in his anger, he fails to remember that there is a giant, rumbling truck over there. He nearly rams into its side before a well-timed horn drops him out of his cloud of fury. The driver makes an obscene hand gesture at John, which of course is just about enough to throw him over the edge.

For the next few minutes, John drives like, well, an idiot. He puts the pedal down whenever he can. He slams on the brakes to avoid collision. He yells at people who can't hear him because his windows are closed, their windows are closed, and it's useless to yell over the cacophony of engines and car horns, anyway. He grinds his teeth. He wrings his hands. He sweats, profusely.

It is then that John looks down at the flashing light on his dashboard. His ridiculously aggressive driving has caused him to begin overheating. His anger shifting suddenly to fear and anxiety, he turns off the radio and the air conditioning and opens his window. For the next few minutes, it's touch and go with his engine. The engine temperature needle begins to drop, but at great expense. John is now burning hot from the lack of air conditioning and he knows that all the way home, his ears will be assaulted by the noise from outside his open windows.

Now, let's examine John's state of mind. He has been presented with a seemingly endless stream of negative triggers. They have in turn spurred in him a ream of typical negative feelings: anger, fear, and anxiety. Unless he makes careful decisions and attempts to calm himself down, he is in no position to continue driving—to say nothing of the condition he will be in when he finally gets home and "greets" his poor family.

But what has John done in this scenario? Has he made decisions based on his negative feelings or has he blindly reacted? The answer is obvious. Actions like gritting his teeth, wringing his hands, honking the horn, cranking up the radio, driving erratically, and, especially, yelling at all those around him as if everyone but himself is to blame—all of these are reactions. None of them solve John's traffic issue. All of them inevitably lead to chaos.

The trouble with this reaction-heavy scenario is that it will extend well beyond John's ninety-minute commute. On top of getting home far later than he had hoped, the agitated father will get home, well, agitated. His anger will bring nothing constructive for his family. He will yell at Jimmy for not having his homework done. He will complain to everyone who will listen about how Jenny is never around. He will groan when he hears that Julie has prepared casserole for dinner. Generally, he will irk everyone in the family to no end.

Television will provide little relief, as his excited state will make him react to every news story in an abundantly negative fashion. His favorite baseball team, in his mind, will play like losers for nine innings (forget the fact that they will wind up winning). And no good news from the family—Jimmy's exceptional quarterly grades, Julie's unusually excellent day, the fact that Jenny is giving serious consideration to trying out for the track team—will do a thing to shake him out of his funk.

How will John sleep? Poorly. How will John wake? Exhausted. How will John's workday look tomorrow? Unproductive. And will John manage to get out of the office at four-thirty? Absolutely not. The cycle of chaos will thus repeat itself.

John Dawson: Calm, Respectful Commuter

Now we won't go into too much detail in this segment, given that Chapter 5 covers at length the nuances of the Decision box, but it is important that we examine the alternative to John's most common set of road rage reactions.

John considers himself a reasonable man. And there was a time not too long ago when he actually *was* a reasonable man. But that was before his job, his commute, and the complexities of family life started to get to him. He now finds himself locked in a seemingly inescapable cycle of chaos. Fortunately for John, a few key decisions, a few reasonable alterations to his life, might lead to more balance on his daily commute.

The simplest decision could be acceptance. Rather than waking up earlier than he should just to avoid the morning gridlock, throwing off the balance of his entire day, he could make a point to accept the fact that it will take him ninety minutes to travel to work and ninety minutes to get home each day. This option works only if John manages to convince himself that those 180 minutes are a blessing rather than a curse. A ninety-minute commute does not have to be a waste of time. These days, not many people get that kind of time to themselves, after all. What does it matter if it happens in the driver's seat of a car?

John could spend his time within his own head, thinking constructively, planning his day at work, resolving his negative feelings about something that happened at home. Thanks to the miracle of recorded word, he could buy a book on tape and catch up on his "reading." He could explore an untapped taste for classical music. He could learn a second language. In this way, his 180 minutes of "wasted" time—time he typically passes by fuming about traffic—become 180 minutes of constructive time.

By refocusing his attention and his understanding of his commute—by *deciding* to take advantage of all that time alone rather than *dreading* all that time in traffic—John will rewire his feelings. He will alter the effect of those thousands of negative triggers. If he is concentrating on a particularly compelling plot turn in his book on tape, that infernal rumbling from the truck to his left will fade out of hearing. If he buries himself in thought, that elderly couple to his right will seem far less annoying and far more comical. If he indulges in the soothing sounds of classical music, the errant braking of the car ahead of him will seem like little more than baroque rhythms in a traffic pattern. And if he focuses his attention on bettering himself, the selfish move of that girl on the cell phone who cut ahead of him will represent nothing more than thirty more seconds in the car to learn the meaning of "tranquilidad."

But the most significant thing that John could do to alter his decision/reaction quotient in relationship to the triggers/feelings that surround him is to *truly* change the environment. The significance of triggers/feelings should not be underestimated. If we choose to operate within environments that feature particularly negative triggers, we are far more likely to fall into a negative pattern of reaction and the chaos it breeds.

If John truly wanted to disembark from his road rage-driven chaos, he could do a number of things to eliminate his commute completely. He could ride a bike to work, for example. It might be a more arduous journey, but given that his job is only ten miles away from his home, it certainly wouldn't take him any longer. In fact, he would carve through traffic and arrive far earlier. And consider the benefits to his health. Twenty miles biking each day would drastically reduce John's body fat index, lowering his stress. It would improve his self-image, again lowering his stress. It would improve his energy levels, freeing him up to do any number of things at work and with his family that he just doesn't seem to have the drive for anymore. He would sleep better. And who *couldn't* use better sleep?

But this isn't an exercise manual. Let's say that John is not a fan of the biking idea. He would rather not spend the money on a bike, he feels it's too great a risk to ride through gridlock, and he really would rather not spend every morning at work dripping with sweat and every afternoon basking in his own stench. No problem. There are certainly other solutions.

John could find a new job, for example. One that's closer to home. One in a direction that requires a route not featuring the interstate or even the bypass. Or if he likes his job too much to leave, perhaps he could use his long tenure there to request the opportunity to work from home. Even a couple of days a week of commuting across the living room floor instead of commuting across the city loop would do wonders for his chaos levels. More time at home might help him iron out some of the family issues that he has been experiencing lately, as well.

As you will see in the coming chapters, then, reasonable, calculated decisions are incredibly powerful. Make no mistake, we are only getting started with this chapter. Read on to discover how truly impactful a decision, rather than a reaction, can be.

Chapter 5

Box 2: Decision

Let's move on now to the second box of our Chaos Model. As has already been mentioned, Box 2 is where the model has the potential to take us in a more favorable direction, one that leads toward balance. In any understanding of the chaos cycle, the goal must be to spend as much time as possible operating within the realm of "Decision" and as little time as possible in the "Reaction" state.

The word "decision" is one that we must examine closely. Most everyone understands it in its grand (and rather vague) sense: the thing that most directly represents those turning points, those crossroads, in one's life. In other words, people generally think of decisions as life-changing events—or at the very least, something significant to have to struggle through.

The word "decision" is usually applied to something huge:

- "Should I take this great new job offer, even though it means having to relocate my family?"
- "Can we afford to send our daughter to an Ivy League school or will she have to go to a state college?"
- "Am I *really* ready to get married?"

You see the point. These are questions that most people don't face every day. They are hard questions. And so we give them a grand name: "decisions." For most, a decision isn't the kind of thing that rules everyday life. We don't call the question of whether we should buy spearmint or wintergreen gum at the gas station a "decision." We call that a "choice." And so it gets sent back into the pack of "little things" that we must deal with on a daily basis.

Further, when faced with a decision, many people think of the decision itself in a negative light. "I've got a difficult decision to make." You hear that one all the time, right? This is simply because, when we're talking about the grand, overarching, life-changing brand of decision, the process of reasoning things out can be rather painful. And at the very least, depending on the decision you make, someone might wind up getting hurt. You can relocate your family in order to advance your career, but then your children would have to make new friends and get accustomed to a new school. Your spouse would have to find a new job or otherwise uproot his/her entire life, as well. Or you could refuse the job offer and condemn your own career to stagnation. A simple, painless answer to this dilemma just doesn't exist. That's a "difficult decision to make."

The trouble with this line of thinking is that not all decisions are difficult. It can certainly be said that not all of them are life-changing. In fact, many decisions are pain-free and can lead to positive change. And many are rather benign. The truth is, we are all faced with dozens of decisions of varying value every day. It's just that most of us don't notice them. They happen too quickly, sometimes without much thought at all. Or they represent a choice we have made long ago—a choice that has become a part of our everyday lifestyle—and so do not require daily thought.

And this is exactly why we must closely examine the Decision box of the model. There are decisions that you have made or are continuing to make that have affected your life in some profound, underlying way. It could be that you have done as John Dawson did and picked a chaos-riddled route to work. It could be that you have chosen to do what his wife, Julie, does: You have significantly overscheduled yourself and your children. It could be that you have relied too heavily on unconscious reactions to daily stress and not nearly enough on conscious decisions.

Regardless of how your decisions are affecting your life, the Chaos Model is designed to help you begin to think *more often* and *more directly* about them. The ultimate goal is for you to become cognizant of all your decisions, big and small. If we can reach the point where you notice and evaluate your decisions in a calm and levelheaded way, you will be ready to conquer the chaos in your life and take that critical step toward balance.

The Life-Altering Brand of Decision

For Julie Dawson, there isn't enough time in a day to do all of the seemingly countless things that she just *has to do*. Lately, as she looks over the calendar hanging next to the refrigerator, she realizes that there isn't even enough time in a *month* to fit in all of life's "demands."

It all began innocently enough. As a young couple, Julie and her husband, John, knew that, financially, life might be a bit difficult in the early going. But money never mattered to either of them nearly as much as the wellbeing of their future children. So when Julie was pregnant with Jenny, the two of them sat down and talked things over. After much deliberation, the first significant decision of Julie's life was made: She would take on the role of stay-at-home mom until Jenny was old enough to go to school. This, they figured, would provide their unborn daughter with a head start on her education—part of Julie's role would be to teach Jenny the kinds of things that children learn in preschool. Julie, meanwhile, could not have been more excited about the opportunity to build a strong bond with her daughter.

In the early years, Julie reveled in her job. She cooked, she cleaned, she taught Jenny her colors and numbers and ABCs. Most importantly, she spent loads of time playing with her daughter. Despite all of this critical work, she always had time for herself in the afternoons (when Jenny was napping), as well. Most often, she would use the time to do one of two things: either keep her mind sharp by staying on top of her reading or check out mentally by tuning in to her favorite afternoon programs. Some days, she would use her afternoons to run errands (when Jenny just didn't want to nap). And on very rare occasions (when Jenny was old enough to attend her Head Start classes), she would treat herself to a massage or get her hair done.

Yes, early on, life was working out for Julie. She might not have envisioned herself as a stay-at-home mom when she was in college, but she quickly discovered that it was not without its advantages. The big decision—what she would do as her career—had already been made. All the little decisions—what to do with all the time in her day—had been put on autopilot, relegated to the hanging calendar on the wall.

You can likely see where this is going. Each year, Julie would buy a new hanging calendar to replace the old one. And each year, that hanging calendar would get more and more cluttered with Julie's increasingly color-coded ink (by the end, the color codes would be crucial; otherwise, it would take extra time to reason out all the notes and obligations to attend to). This was the first sign that Julie's decisions had begun to devolve into chaos-driven reactions—more on this point later.

First, let's examine the cause of this devolution…

As Jenny got older, Julie grew more and more excited about the opportunity to pursue a different career. She had studied accounting in college, and so was looking forward to getting back to the numbers that had so driven her in her youth. Besides, she felt that it would be nice to contribute to the family financially for a change. But by the time Jenny reached school age, Julie was pregnant with Jimmy. While she had been enjoying her time at home with her daughter—and was certainly thrilled about how close she and Jenny had become—she couldn't help but feel a little slighted when her husband suggested that she continue her life at home until Jimmy reached school age.

"It just wouldn't be fair to Jimmy," John reasoned.

Julie remembers thinking that her husband was absolutely right. She couldn't get a job now. She owed it to Jimmy. So the second major decision was made…

The Hanging Calendar: The Ultimate Chaos Generator

These days, even with both of her children in school, Julie's life lacks the kind of balance it had when Jenny was just a toddler. Every day is a struggle for this increasingly stressed stay-at-home mom, in fact. Waking Jenny is a chore. Dressing Jimmy is a chore. Making breakfast and packing lunches is a chore. Shopping is a chore. Yoga class is a chore. Carting the kids around to their seemingly endless obligations is a chore—driving *anywhere* is a chore. Cooking for the family is a chore. Even all of the things that Julie used to do to unwind have started to seem like a chore.

In short, Julie is miserable. And as she would tell you, it isn't because she has lost interest in being a stay-at-home mom. In fact, over the years, she has become rather comfortable in her position at home. She can't imagine doing anything else.

Still, there is a part of Julie that regrets not pursuing the accounting career that she had studied for. Indeed, there is a part of her that feels a little guilty about not following the women's liberation path that she had so subscribed to in her youth. What she has done to compensate for this guilt—

in other words, how she has demonstrated a chaotic reaction to this guilt—is to turn to her hanging calendar. More and more, Julie feels obligated to justify every minute of her day. Her need for justification has come so far, in fact, that she has begun to schedule appointments for her children that overlap. She has taken things to the point where she must occasionally be in two places at once.

A look at this dreadful hanging calendar is quite revealing. It is so complicated as to need a labeling key to decipher. The blue ink signifies Jimmy's obligations: field trip, guitar lessons, soccer practice, Boy Scouts meeting, a dentist appointment. The pink ink is for Jenny: state mandated exams, volleyball practice (though this note only remains on the calendar because it was written at the start of the year; Jenny has since quit most of her social obligations), student council dinner, dance class, a dentist appointment, a doctor appointment. Then there's brown for John: work, client luncheon, poker night, business trip, soccer practice (he's Jimmy's coach), a dentist appointment, a doctor appointment.

And all of this fits (or doesn't fit, depending on your perspective) within one week. Many of the obligations listed above are daily, as well. Each week is plenty cluttered with blue, pink, and brown notations.

The rest of the calendar is littered with notes in green. These denote Julie's responsibilities. To read them is like reading the longest to-do list ever assembled. There are daily tasks: wake Jenny, dress Jimmy, make breakfast, prepare lunches, dishes, shop, cook dinner. There are semi-daily tasks: drive Jenny to dance, work out, pick Jimmy up from guitar lessons. There are weekly tasks: clean, call Mom, pay electric bill, volunteer at school, do laundry. And there are random tasks: dentist, doctor, cook meal for student council dinner, drive John to airport.

In the end, there is almost no white space for additional notes. The notes are so jumbled and numerous that reading the calendar qualifies as a chore all its own.

The Chaos Reaction

Julie is so overcommitted and has stretched herself so thin that she often has to drop her children off at their practices or appointments late. In addition, she is constantly forgetting about things that she has scheduled her family for. She can't remember the last time she had an hour alone to read, watch TV, or just unwind. Forget about massage or hair appointments. Those rare treats seem like ancient history at this point. And (in her mind) worse yet, she is so overbooked that she doesn't even have time to do the cleaning around the house anymore. She is giving serious thought to hiring a maid.

Lately, this has bred an altogether unwelcome reaction in Julie—and nobody loathes it more than Julie herself: impatience. She snaps at her daughter when she doesn't wake up right away. She frantically dresses her son (to the point where his dread of actually getting dressed is probably the real reason why he's not dressing himself at nine years old in the first place). She grumbles through breakfast, harping on her children to remember all that they have to do during the upcoming day. She spends her entire day alone in a rush. The occasional run-in with a friend at the supermarket or the post office is now viewed as a nuisance, where once it was an unexpected joy. There just doesn't seem to be enough time to cram in all that Julie *needs* to do.

So Julie reacts to her impossible daily routine with frustration and anger. She is short with her children and even shorter with her husband. As a result—and coupled with John's own shortening fuse—the marriage has grown strained. A strained marriage, of course, leads to more stress, which in turn leads to more pressure on Jimmy and Jenny. The cycle churns and builds upon itself.

While all of this certainly leads to a great deal of chaos for Julie, the above point is especially important to note: It also rubs off on her children. As we will see, Jenny has turned to drugs to help deal with the stress of her daily routine. And Jimmy, only nine years old, is already starting to forget what it means to be a kid—he no longer has unstructured time to himself, with his friends, or even for play.

Julie must confess that she has overbooked herself unconsciously. But she knows why she has done it. Her guilt for not pursuing her business career has led her to *need* to justify everything that she does as a mother. If she can't be a qualified accountant, then she feels the need to be Supermom. As a result, all of her energy is poured into her children and her husband. There is absolutely no time left for her to take care of herself.

The end result? Constant stress for Julie, constant stress for the entire family. The epitome of chaos. There is no balance in Julie's life whatsoever. Between the over scheduling and under-relaxing embarked upon by her family, there is no balance there, either.

Undoing the Environment of Chaos

Make no mistake, it is not my intention to place all of the blame for the Dawson family's chaos on Julie. Certainly, the other three play equally significant parts (particularly John, with his constant yelling and his all-too-lofty expectations). But Julie's reactions, her need to over schedule, aren't helping her own chaos versus balance picture. Being the backbone of the family—the one who truly brings everyone together, both literally and figuratively—it is perhaps her level of chaos that stands as the most important for the group. If she demonstrates balance in her life, then the children will demonstrate balance. If chaos, then chaos. Of course, John must also demonstrate balance if the family hopes to improve, but in the end, it all goes hand in hand.

So this is the trouble for Julie: Her need to over schedule isn't a decision, it's a reaction. Instead of booking herself to cook a student council dinner while simultaneously driving Jimmy to soccer practice and Jenny to dance practice (an impossible feat for anyone), she might try taking steps to let go of a few of the unnecessary obligations. There is no need for a mom—even Supermom—to be everywhere at once. There is no need to structure a child's entire day. And there is no need to play secretary for a spouse.

If Julie hopes to right her own chaos versus balance equation, her first step is a simple one: She must throw out that awful calendar. Granted, calendars can be useful, as some structure is certainly important—but that old calendar, with all its marks and scribbles, has got to go. She could start fresh with a brand new calendar with plenty of white space.

Now, as she moves forward and begins filling out her new schedule, the first thing she should omit is John's obligations. John is a grown man (with his own calendar at work) and can take care of his own responsibilities. Next, she should uncover all of the points where she has booked herself to be in two places at once. In these cases, she should either relegate more responsibility to John or cancel the conflicting obligations.

But more important than all of that is what Julie needs to do for herself. If she is addicted to scheduling, then she *must* make a point to schedule a reasonable amount of time for herself. It doesn't matter what she does, just so long as it is something that will allow her to unwind. It is time for her to begin scheduling that regular massage again. Time for hair appointments. Time for reading and television. Time for meditation and hot baths.

When she was younger, Julie decided that she would be a stay-at-home mom—and it was a decision that would bring her years of happiness. But when the happiness faded to resentment and guilt, she *reacted* by over-booking herself. Now she stands in a whirlpool of chaos. The only way out is for Julie to make a conscious *decision* to restructure her life. She must take down that calendar and write a new one. She must realize that her own sanity, her own balance, is every bit as important to the family's health and wellbeing as Jenny's volleyball practice or Jimmy's dentist appointment or John's poker night.

Decisions, Decisions

If anything about Julie's story sounds like you, then you must recognize it as a sign: You must work to pay better attention to your daily decisions. The truest path to a balanced life is to make calculated and beneficial decisions about how to live and behave. In Julie's case, a big decision—to continue on as a stay-at-home mom many years after she was originally willing to do so—led to a series of smaller decisions—to book herself and her children for a ridiculous number of responsibilities—which in turn led to a slew of chaos-driven reactions—bickering with the kids, struggling with daily obligations, arguing with her increasingly irritable husband, etc.

In much the same way, many people's lives follow the same path. We occasionally find ourselves in jobs that we hate, so we bury ourselves in structured social activities that we believe will make us happier and fuller individuals. But when the activities fail to do what we had hoped, or when we feel that the competition is gaining some sort of advantage on us, we react. And how do we react? We add more activities. Then more. Then more. And so on. In the end, we wind up so overburdened that the activities themselves begin to feel like chores.

The fact that our former pleasures have turned into pains leads to another common reaction: stress and irritability. Many of our life's most important aspects—our families, our friends, and (ironically) our jobs—wind up suffering because we have given ourselves far too much to do.

If we hope to break this cycle of chaos, if we hope to move away from our reaction-driven lifestyles, we must make a conscious effort to decide what we need and do not need in order to be happy. We must determine the best balance for our work and play, for our obligations and our pleasurable distractions.

But all of this goes well beyond scheduling. In your own life, there are hundreds of triggers/feelings that you encounter every day. For John, it is road rage. For Julie, it is a lack of fulfillment from her work. It does not matter what brings us to the point of decision versus reaction, balance versus chaos. All that matters is which path we choose.

Think about your own life for a moment. Consider your latest dilemma. It could be something as significant as a new job offer or insignificant as whether to sacrifice two hours of sleep to watch a movie. In any case, there was a point when you were presented with a decision ("Do I take the new job?" or "Can I afford only five hours of sleep tonight?"). In order to get a handle on a chaos addiction, one must learn to make a conscious decision instead of an unconscious reaction (the chaos-addicted individual might take the new job because it pays better, even if it means uprooting his/her whole family and generally making life more difficult; and the chaos-addicted individual has no trouble justifying the sacrifice of sleep, regardless of the consequences).

As we move through the next two chapters, you will get a firsthand look at how reaction can lead to a life of chaos. But for now, let's examine a few common dilemmas and discuss the kinds of decisions that can bring an otherwise stressful environment back into balance.

Chapter 6

Box 3: Reaction

So you now have a deeper understanding of the "Decision" path of the Chaos Model. It is important to remember that decisions, while often difficult, are things that we always have control over in our lives. It may surprise some to think that we also have control over the next box of the model, Reaction.

Unlike decisions—which are more cerebral and exist almost entirely in our conscious mind—reactions are born of our baser instincts. Many times, a reaction is designed simply to help us avoid pain. Pain of all sorts. The stressors in our lives—the things that cause us to feel overwhelmed, create sadness, or even generate feelings of inadequacy—can directly lead to pain. It is how we respond to that stress, that pain, that leads us either in the direction of balance or chaos.

As you learned in the previous chapter, making conscious and calculated decisions about how to deal with your daily life and the stress that it may cause is the most direct way to avoid chaos. If you take the time to make careful decisions about how to conduct yourself, your life will certainly find more balance. But if you allow your reactions to take over—something that we seem to find ourselves doing more and more these days—then you are likely on your way to a chaotic life (if you are not there already). If feelings of stress or anxiety are allowed to trigger reactions, then those reactions will fuel your level of chaos. The chaos, in turn, will lead to more stress or anxiety. And the cycle perpetuates itself. What is more, the cycle *builds upon* itself. The more time we spend in the reaction state, the more chaos we will find in our lives.

So what is a reaction? How do we spot them when they occur? As mentioned, a reaction can be aligned with what we also refer to as instincts. So if we look at things from that perspective, the picture becomes clearer. One of the most well-known instincts is called the "fight or flight" reaction. What it means is that when we are threatened by something (whether it be another person, a particular problem, or the very environment in which we live), our first instinct, our first reaction, falls into one of two categories: either we fight back against the trigger that makes us feel this way or we "fly" from it. Basically, if we feel that our best course of action is to struggle against something, then we struggle against it, regardless of what it might do to us emotionally or physically. If we feel that we cannot possibly win the battle— that no matter what we do, we will wind up losing to the stressor in the end—then we run.

Now if we are talking about animals in nature, then the fight or flight reaction is quite literal. If an animal is attacked, it will either fight back or run away. But since we are such complex animals, for us, fight or flight is much more complicated. There are, of course, many ways for a person to fight and many ways for a person to run.

With the following story of Jenny Dawson, we will learn about several of the most common.

The Fighter

Jenny finds herself in a very precarious situation: In her life, there are many triggers that she encounters on a daily basis. But that is not what makes her unique in the Dawson family. All of the Dawsons, after all, encounter many triggers each day. It is just that, at seventeen years old, Jenny is at an age when she is both old enough to be cognizant of her triggers and young enough to not know how to deal with them. This being the case, she very often trends toward her baser instincts, toward reactions rather than decisions, regarding her perceived problems.

It is hard to blame Jenny for either fighting or running. In terms of a childhood, her entire life has been comparatively overwhelming. From the time she entered high school, she was expected by her enterprising parents to achieve a 4.0 grade point average. "You want to be able to choose whatever college you like, don't you?" her parents would always ask her. "Then you need to get straight A's."

As if that were not enough (and with all the homework that children receive nowadays, achieving a 4.0 seems like a monumental task), Jenny was also expected to be a top athlete (in three sports, no less!), a talented musician, and a sublime dancer. Just imagine trying to fit all of that in one day, let alone excel in every facet.

To Jenny's great credit, for nearly two years she did keep up with this incredibly heavy load. She would go to school—taking detailed notes and paying attention diligently—work hard at practice, complete her mountain of homework, and then finish the day by practicing her latest dance routine or flute lesson. For a while, she even enjoyed taking all of this on at once. She used to tell herself that she hated being bored. To her, it seemed as if she had two choices: either she worked hard during every minute of the day, or she sat around bored, staring at the television.

But Jenny's schedule is not solely to blame. As mentioned, when Jenny began experimenting with drugs, she was only fifteen. At this time, it can be said that she was both too young to make the proper decision about such things and plenty old enough to perceive another common stressor in the lives of children these days. For Jenny, the increasing strain between her mother and father—something most likely caused by John's stress at work and Julie's lack of fulfillment at home—seemed almost tangible. Unlike young Jimmy, who remained relatively oblivious to his parents' marital troubles, Jenny experienced the turmoil directly. She could sense when her mother and father were not getting along, even if John and Julie did their best to hide it. She could take on the stress associated with John's daily commute and career frustration. She could feel the anguish of her mother, both overbooked and under-satisfied.

So here is Jenny: old enough to sense the strain on her family, young enough to assume that it was all her fault. What did she do in reaction? At first, she tried working harder at everything. No grade was high enough. No good play on the court was good enough. No slip-up on stage, however minor, would go unpunished.

Well, as she got older, the work stress and the family stress began to wear on her. What's more, she was exposed to a number of other things that completely disproved her work-or-be-bored theory. Her friends always seemed to be having fun, after all, whereas her daily schedule (now an incredible chore) was anything but fun.

It was at the age of sixteen when things began to fall apart for Jenny.

This was the age when she began to fall back on her reactions. Her first reaction? Fight. And fight she did. Against her parents, her teachers, her coaches, her friends. Everyone in Jenny's life began to get a little uncomfortable. Jenny, once such a sweet girl, had become extremely irritable. About *everything*. If she got a B on an exam, she would argue. If her parents would not let her borrow the car to go to a movie on a Saturday night, she would argue. If her brother beat her to the bathroom in the morning, she would argue. If her friends had other plans during her rare moments of free time, she would argue. Things were getting ugly.

But no one ever did anything constructive about it. Everyone simply fought back. Most people told Jenny that she was being unreasonable or unfair, or that she was just being mean. So, eventually, it began to look to Jenny like fighting just wasn't going to cut it. She had to find another way out. So she turned to perhaps the most destructive of all reactions: the one that calls for running away from one's problems.

The Runner

Jenny was desperate—desperate to be accepted by her new friends (her old friends had turned their backs on her because she had been so pushy and argumentative lately). Desperate to find some outlet for all of her anger. Desperate to make her parents feel exactly the way she did (miserable). Desperate to unplug from her incredibly demanding life. Desperate to have fun.

Regardless of who we are or where we come from, we can all identify with desperation. It causes us to do some very silly things. We react poorly, taking the easy way out, and those reactions lead to trouble. For Jenny, the easy way out was not to reexamine her workload. It was not to recognize her own anger, her own fight reaction, and mend all the bridges she had burned with her friends, family, teachers, and coaches. All of these things would have taken decisions. And the right decisions, especially for a seventeen-year-old, are often difficult to make.

No, for Jenny, the flight reaction represented the easy way out. In this case, the flight reaction began with avoiding school. At first, she would just "forget" to do homework or study for a test. Eventually, she would start skipping school altogether. She would run away from more of her responsibilities on the day she quit the basketball team. She would do this, of course, without telling her parents (and the day they would find out would end in an epic fight). The act of dropping dancing and music lessons represented further running on Jenny's part. But none of these flights, these reactions, were as damaging as the very thing that caused her to do all of this in the first place.

Jenny's initial reaction—her first instinct when it came to "unplugging" from her stressful life—was to do as her new friends were doing: experiment with drugs. It began with marijuana. She found that this helped her relax and enjoy the company of her new friends, for a change. But when that didn't completely solve her problems with her parents (in fact, if anything, it made her stress at home even worse), she graduated to harder and more serious drugs.

These days, Jenny—once such a promising, bright, talented, and pretty young lady—is a D student with little ambition, almost no respect for authority, and a girl who possesses literally no joy in her life. More troubling is the fact that she now teeters dangerously close to an addiction to methamphetamine, the latest drug of choice for her and her friends.

In summary, Jenny has run away from all of her problems by turning to drugs. She has circumvented all of her triggers simply by ignoring them and concentrating on an outlet that does little more than numb her to everything that she used to consider important. She does not want to hate her parents. She does not want poor grades. She does not want to spend all of her days and nights doing nothing but getting high. But now she has no choice. She has run so far that she cannot stop running. At least, not without help. The reaction, the running, has itself become chaos. And as far as Jenny is concerned, there does not seem to be any way out.

Reactions, Reactions

Addiction is a nasty thing. And it is always born of reaction. Nobody ever *decides* to be addicted to drugs or alcohol. They just find themselves retreating to the habit. As we have covered already, addictions to things such as drugs and alcohol have as much to do with a chaos addiction than anything else we may encounter in our lives. Jenny Dawson is the perfect example. It was not a conscious decision that led her to try drugs. It was her original addiction to chaos—her perceived need to be the perfect student, the perfect athlete, the perfect musician and dancer. As her life became more and more chaotic, she increasingly felt the need to over-commit herself. And when that life got to be too much, she reacted, and eventually developed the ultimate symptom of chaos addiction: drug addiction.

For Jenny, if she continues to operate in this reaction state—continues to fuel her chaos at even greater levels—then she is headed for trouble. There is the obvious physical and social turmoil that drugs will lead her to: Her relationship with her parents will grow even more strained, the people in her life (including her friends) will become alienated by her devolving personality, her grades will continue to slip (to the point where she might not even grad-uate from high school, which would, of course, lead to any number of other social consequences, all of them contributing to more chaos), and her body will succumb to all of the tremendous health risks associated with drug use. Worse yet, there will come a time when Jenny will need to run away from her problems, and drugs alone will not suffice. When this occurs, other addictions may boil to the surface—all of them a direct result of Jenny's underlying addiction to chaos.

At only seventeen, if Jenny does not seek ways to find more balance in her life, she could find herself in rehab. She could wind up experimenting with sex—and at that age, with such little perceived emotional support in her life, experimentation could easily become another dangerous addiction. In the end, regardless of where her reaction path takes her, she will wind up with a life far more chaotic than the one she started running from in the first place. She will fall into a spiral of chaos from which there seems no escape.

Deciding to Eliminate Addiction

While the statistics regarding drug use in this country (particularly drug use on the part of children) are staggering, drug addiction still represents an extreme in the chaos cycle. Not everyone addicted to chaos winds up addicted to drugs or alcohol or gambling or sex. But even if you do not display one of these more physical manifestations of addiction, you must understand that there is plenty for you to identify with and learn from in Jenny's story.

For one thing, Jenny teaches the lesson that living at the behest of your reactions is a dangerous road to travel. Unfortunately, almost all of us react to triggers/feelings every day. While we may not turn to drug use to run away from our troubles at school, work, or home, there are certainly other potentially damaging outlets to fall into. Television, for example, can be an addiction. How many of us watch more than three hours of TV every night? How much of that time could be spent doing something a little more constructive, something that brings more balance into our lives? Other people tune out by joining the virtual realm of the Internet, spending hours obsessing about fantasy sports or role-playing games or fictional commu-nities. Many others delve into videogames.

You see the point. Addiction can come from anywhere. Regardless of the addiction, it likely springs out of an addiction to chaos, a subconscious need to keep our lives spinning out of balance. If we hope to treat the presenting addiction, it is not enough to recommend watching less TV, spending more time with the family, or checking into rehab. Instead, we must determine the best ways to get the chaos addict thinking more about his/her decisions and spending less time in the reaction phase.

In Jenny's case, reaction has dictated much of her adolescence. To get her back on the right track is no easy task. Her primary reaction—to fight with everyone in her life—led to a series of destructive consequences: increased strain on the family, a loss of friends, and the breakdown of her school and extracurricular performance. Her secondary reaction—to run away from her problems by turning to drugs—led to a series of even more destructive consequences: more strain on family and friends, the near ruin of her entire school career, the tremendous damage done to her body and mind, and the potential to develop additional (and equally dangerous) addictions in her life.

Just like Jenny, many of us find ourselves overburdened. Additionally, there are few families without at least a few dysfunctions. It is a harsh reality. In reaction, we keep ourselves distracted with a number of activities designed to unplug from that reality. For Jenny, it was drugs. For another, it might be gambling. For still another, it might be taking on a series of destructive relationships. But when these addictions fail to keep us fully separated from our problems (and they often do fail, eventually), we react again. The reaction? We develop more and different addictions.

Addiction is a double-edged sword. While the substance or activity that we are addicted to might bring us short-term pleasure, it almost always leads to long-term pain. Everything in our lives winds up suffering from this pain as a result. There is a name for this suffering: chaos. This is chaos at work.

In today's society, the first so-called remedy to addiction is to attend rehab. In some cases, drugs are prescribed to help the individual cope with the loss of the thing they once felt they needed. Unfortunately, this remedy does not always work. Too many people spend their lives in and out of rehab. Too many people wind up addicted to the very drugs that were supposed to help them beat addiction.

So why do our most prevalent solutions fail? Because the presenting addiction is not the problem, it is the symptom. The central problem is an addiction to chaos. And as you have learned, the only way to treat a chaos addiction is to work toward solutions to bring balance into your life. How is that done? By spending more time deciding and less time reacting.

In Jenny's case, when she first began to feel overwhelmed (her first true trigger/feeling), she could have made a number of decisions that would have kept her from falling into drug addiction: She could have looked at her over-whelming schedule and picked a few things to drop—this way, she'd find the time she needed to have fun and be a sixteen-year-old kid for a change. Soft-ball could have been cut. As could dancing. She could have spent her summers relaxing at home or spending time with friends instead of signing up for summer camp after summer camp. Jenny had long since gotten bored of these activities, anyway.

As for her parents—and the stress that their decomposing marriage brought to their daughter's life—there is no reason that Jenny could not have confronted John and Julie rather than suppressed her feelings about the matter. If she had taken the time to sit down with her mother and father and explain that she felt they had a problem, everyone might have been better for it. Jenny's decision to take action would have helped her alleviate some of her own family-related stress. She would have learned that she herself was not to blame. And for Julie and John, hearing about their strained marriage from their only daughter might have been just the wake-up call they needed to try to work things out.

Think about your own life for a moment. Consider your ongoing dilemmas. Like Julie and Jenny, you could be too busy for your taste. Like John and Julie, you might find stress at home. Like John, you may hate your job or your commute. Now, ask yourself this question: How do you *deal with* these ongoing problems?

The answer is obvious: You react to them. How can this be claimed with such certainty? Because if you had already taken the time to *decide* on solu-tions to these ongoing problems, then they wouldn't be ongoing. You would not be in a position of chaos. Your life would have perfect balance.

Of course, no one has perfect balance. The goal of the Chaos Model is to help you add *more* balance to your life, regardless of where you stand. But before we can demonstrate exactly how to work toward balance, we must take a look at the clearest picture of chaos yet in the Dawson family. And the bad news is that it comes from the age group most at risk of devel-oping chaos addiction: the youngest among us.

Chapter 7

Box 4: Chaos

This brings us to our dreaded final box: Chaos. As you may have seen, this is the easiest box in which to find oneself. Because of this factor, it is also the box in which most people spend the bulk of their lives operating. Spend too much time in this state and you may find that you become locked in a chaos addiction.

If you find that your life feels constantly out of balance, that you feel overwhelmed by stress all the time, that you constantly feel as if you are being pulled in multiple directions at once, then you have too much chaos in your life. If you are always short of energy, always feel irritable, find that you are losing interest in your goals and relationships, and it seems as if no matter what you do, things always end up going wrong, then you must consider strategies to help bring more balance into your life. These strategies will be outlined thoroughly in Chapter 8, but for now, let's take a look at the power of chaos. Let's examine the story of a young boy who has no choice but to live in this most damaging box of the Chaos Model.

Jimmy Dawson: The Boy Raised on Chaos

We have covered three boxes of the Chaos Model. And to this point, we have examined the stories of three people from the same family in order to highlight the telling signs associated with each box. And that leaves us with young Jimmy, a boy growing up in an environment riddled with chaos. The three people whom Jimmy looks up to most—the ones he studies both consciously and subconsciously every day—are setting a terrible example for the boy to follow. The result? Increasingly, Jimmy is taking what he has learned with him to school.

Jimmy's day begins bright and early in the morning, when his aggravated father wakes him before heading off to work. An argument usually follows. See, Jimmy used to be quite good about getting up—he used to love school, after all—but, lately, he just can't seem to find the energy to tear himself out of bed. The argument that kicks off almost every day for Jimmy is about one of two things: either his dad screams at him for not getting up when called or he barks at him about the homework that he failed to finish the previous night. If it is the former, Jimmy wakes exhausted and angry at his father. If it is the latter, Jimmy wakes stressed about his homework and, yes, still angry at his father.

From there, Jimmy heads down the stairs, where he is greeted by another chaotic environment. His mother, looking disheveled and anxious, rushes between packing Jimmy's lunch and preparing breakfast. There was a time when breakfast was a relaxing routine for the whole family. A time when everyone could gather to laugh and converse about their upcoming days. But those days are long gone. Now, Jimmy gets reminded about the homework that he still has to finish (by his curt mother, this time). He has to rifle through his bag (and on the days when he's misplaced his bag and can't find it, all hell breaks loose) for his books and drops them on the table. Breakfast, for him, is now nothing more than a distraction from the work he has to do.

Typically, he completes all of these tasks—homework, eating, answering his mother's incessant questions about school and his evening obligations, and repacking his bag—under the watchful glare of his increasingly distant and silent sister. A year or two earlier, Jenny and Jimmy had been best friends. Despite their significant difference in age (or perhaps *because* of it), they had seemed nearly inseparable. Jenny would always invite her little brother to join her in things: watching TV, playing in the yard, even going to the mall. But ever since Jenny got her license and started her own sordid life, a rift had formed between her and her brother. This had a clear effect on Jimmy. His parents had noticed it, but they were obviously too busy with all of their obligations to do anything about it.

For a year or so, school had been a place of solace for Jimmy. But as you already know, that has changed lately. Between being bullied on the bus and playground, and the mountains of homework that he receives at school, the confused little boy has nowhere to turn. His free time is no help, either, as it is little more than another pile of obligations for him to worry about.

The result? Jimmy carries his stress around with him everywhere. His grades are slipping. His interest in sports is waning. His desire to play the guitar has almost completely evaporated. And worse yet, his relationships with everyone in his life are deteriorating. Where he used to be playful and energetic, he is now irritable and lazy. It has gotten to the point where he wants nothing more than to spend every moment of his free time plugging in to the television or his videogames (and his taste in these games has become increasingly violent, as well). It is all that his parents can do to wrench him away from the TV.

Obviously, this addiction to TV and videogames only exacerbates Jimmy's problem. Each day, he wakes up with even more homework that he failed to finish the night before. As the mornings pile up, his dad gets angrier and angrier. The angrier his father gets (and the higher his stack of homework), the more stressed and aggravated Jimmy feels. And the cycle continues, churning out more chaotic fire with each completed loop.

So Jimmy is headed for a chaos addiction. And all of this at the tender age of nine. But that is not even the worst part. The worst part is that Jimmy, being a nine-year-old, has no way out. Everyone and everything he knows contributes directly to his chaos addiction. For him, the very act of growing up is learning how to lead a life of chaos.

Chaos and Children

The current generation of children is in trouble for the same reason that Jimmy is in trouble: The addiction to chaos starts in childhood. To alleviate the problem, parents need to get to know the dynamics of childhood in order to understand the chaos addiction that might be resulting. Children are much more susceptible to addiction—they simply do not have the sophisticated defense mechanisms of an adult. In addition, stress is just not as understandable to them. So they cannot grasp and deal with the concept of it like adults can. They cannot look at their lives and say, "Boy, I am really stressed out. I should take a vacation."

Instead, children deal with stress by modeling their behavior after their parents and siblings. This reactionary reflex cannot be helped. It is just how children operate—and for good reason. This is how we all learn and grow and become functioning adults. Unfortunately, even if the model of behavior that they are exposed to is negative, children still emulate that model. If they grow up surrounded by chaos, then they will create chaotic environments for themselves when they reach adulthood.

Is every child at risk? Of course not. Is every child the same? Of course not. Children often react in different ways to what they are feeling about the world. But this is exactly why the concept of stress and chaos in their lives is so particularly dangerous. We simply cannot predict the occurrence and intensity of a child's stress. Further, when a child is stressed, we cannot really be sure how he might react. For instance, siblings may respond differently to constant fighting between their parents. Whereas one may tune out, another may show signs of stress by fidgeting or becoming hyperactive at school. The Dawson family is the perfect example. Jenny tunes out with drugs; Jimmy lashes out with a combination of hyperactivity and indifference.

As we learned earlier, parents and people in positions of authority in most children's lives are increasingly looking at the behaviors as problems rather than symptoms. It is important as parents to note that the behavior is only a reaction to what the child is feeling. The behavior is the *outlet*, not the *issue*. Fidgeting, squirming, and appearing distracted can be a model of hyperactivity. But it can also be a model of stress and chaos. Daydreaming can work both ways, as well. This technique is often used by children attempting to disengage from a chaotic environment, whether it be at home or at school. When a child lives continuously in chaos, he/she must build up a defense against it. And these defenses come out as less savory modes of behavior.

In my practice, I counseled a six-year-old female who had what I call a reactionary parent. Reactionary individuals are those who operate most often in Box 3 of the Chaos Model—they tend to respond to situations without taking into account the whole picture. In this instance, the parent in question would respond to the child harshly, regardless of the situation. She would yell, refer to the child with degrading names, lash out for no particular reason. She even accused her child of causing her divorce, claiming that she was "lucky" to even be allowed to live under her mother's roof.

Obviously, not all parents are like this. What we are seeing in this case is an extreme example. But the interesting thing to note is that this six-year-old girl now exhibits exactly the same behavior as her mother. She yells at other children, becomes overly aggressive, shows a lack of boundaries, and makes fun of other people whenever she can. In other words, she is modeling exactly what has been taught to her by her parent. That being the case, one has to wonder whether we should really hold the child accountable for this kind of behavior…

A child who grows up in an atmosphere like this one usually begins to initiate his/her own chaos. When faced with a trigger/feeling, he/she goes right into a reaction response. He/she has no choice, because reaction is all that has been learned. Just as problem solving and decision-making are learned behaviors, so too is reactive behavior. Children living in chaotic families will not learn these more favorable behaviors—they will not learn self-control or discipline—until well after they are labeled in their social environments. In other words, before a child can come to terms with how to decide on things, that child will have long since been labeled according to the time they spent in the reaction state. These labels are difficult if not impossible to escape. If a child is labeled ADHD because of his/her hyperactive behavior in school, for example, even when he/she outgrows that need to be hyperactive, he/she will still be considered ADHD.

This is truly an injustice to children. And the only way out is to fix the chaos before it leads to a behavior problem. Unless children are taught to understand feelings and given appropriate behavior outlets, they will continue to build social foundations upon reaction. Their lives will revolve around anger, fear, stress, and a complete lack of self-control.

The problem is only getting worse. One only needs to pick up a newspaper to validate this statement. Children, it seems, are becoming angrier and more aggressive. Chaotic homes depict violence and fear-evoking situations, which in turn leads to reactionary behavior outside the home. This is very apparent as we read the horror stories of shootings on school grounds, at malls, and even in daycare centers. And worse yet, when something like this occurs, the parents and teachers of these children respond with even more damaging reactionary behavior.

Consider Columbine. Recall the children screaming and running from the school building. They were filed out to be questioned and cared for by medical personnel, then finally swept up into the arms of their parents. What happened then? Those who survived the shooting were provided with crisis counselors. The school also set up metal detectors to prevent guns from getting on the grounds in the future. Could these measures have been implemented before the shooting even occurred? Of course they could have. But the cost, at the time, had been considered too high.

I do not mean to suggest that Columbine High School did not adequately protect its students from such a threat. How could I? Before Columbine, it would have been unlikely to imagine that such a threat even existed. The point here is that, as a society, we have a tendency to react to crisis situations rather than make decisions about them. When children were shot in Colorado, the reaction was to counsel the survivors and lock down the school. What do these two actions generate? More fear. More distrust. More chaos.

Since so many of us as parents are not focused on being proactive as it pertains to chaos in the life of a child, we leave these same children in fear of one another. Modeling prevention and proper problem solving tends to have a longer-lasting effect than knee-jerk reaction to a crisis. Teaching a child to seek balance and rationalize ways to solve his/her problems is far better than making him/her pass through a metal detector on the way in to school.

In the Dawson family, there is only so much that Jimmy and Jenny can do to work their way out of their chaos addictions without help from their parents. Ultimately, it is John and Julie's responsibility to provide a calm atmosphere in which their children can thrive, learn, relax, and feel safe. But if John and Julie continue to fight with each other and with their children on a constant basis, there will be nowhere for their children to turn in search of calm. If Julie continues to tell Jenny one thing about her friends while her father continues to tell her another, there is nowhere to turn for the consistency that a child needs to build trust. If Jimmy is told to finish his homework and then forced to go to guitar lessons, he loses his opportunity to have fun. Eventually, the concept of fun will be lost to him.

All of this produces fear in a child. Fear then becomes chaos. And that chaos is carried into adulthood.

The Signs and Symptoms of Chaos

Now that we have a better understanding of what it is like to live in chaos and where that chaos likely comes from, we may move on to uncover how you can identify whether you have too much chaos in your own life. Remember, even if you feel that you have everything under control, you may be experiencing chaos that you do not recognize.

The main symptom of chaos is the inability to stop creating negative situations, *no matter what you do*. If you find that whenever you get past one stressful or chaotic situation, you fall immediately into another, then the situations themselves may be self-induced. In other words, you may be so addicted to chaos that you subconsciously *create* chaotic situations just to feel normal. People who fall into this category most often become addicted to other, more tangible things as well (such as drugs, alcohol, sex, or gambling).

But alternate addiction is only one defense mechanism for the chaos addict. In fact, those addicted to chaos may develop an entire array of defenses to justify their chaotic lives. They might deliberately get into arguments or even physical fights. They may break off engagements even if they don't want to (say, for example, that you claimed you would be home at nine, but stayed out until eleven even though you had every opportunity and desire to be home at nine). They might act foolishly or change their personalities whenever they become uncomfortable. They may complain about how unmanageable and undesirable their lives are while simultaneously claiming, "This is who I am and there is nothing wrong with me." They might develop an interest in dangerous hobbies or behaviors (think motorcycle racing or extreme sports). They may begin committing crimes regardless of need or desperation (think shoplifting when you have the money to pay for something). Or they might begin engaging in sexually reckless behavior.

Even if you can read that entire paragraph and say, "None of those descriptions sound like me," that does not necessarily mean that you are not addicted to chaos. Not everyone demonstrates chaotic behavior in the same way. And in addition to all of that, another prime symptom of chaos is denial.

So ask yourself these questions:

- Have I done things I could have gotten arrested for?
- Have I chosen friends who have either been arrested in the past or regularly partake in activities that could get them arrested?
- Am I attracted to illegal activities?
- Have I been involved in an affair?
- Have I ever stolen from friends?
- Have I ever lied for no real reason?
- Have I ever spent money recklessly?
- Have I ever been sexually reckless?
- Have I ever lost my job?
- Am I sick more often than most?
- Has my recklessness ever cost the people in my life money?

Chaos addicts often put insurmountable stress on their relationships. Family members, friends, significant others—all of them wind up hurt or alienated. The chaos addicts repeat the same cycles of behavior when it comes to relationships, always wondering why they end up with the same types of people or the same types of problems with those people. This cycle manifests itself in moodiness, broken promises, money problems, and even violence. The addiction leads even the most caring individuals to become more selfish. Many times, close, personal values are compromised. Even spirituality evaporates under the light of chaos.

As you can see, living in Box 4 of the Chaos Model can be a very dangerous thing. Even if you found yourself answering "no" to most of the questions presented in this chapter, even if you find that your life is only occasionally chaotic, you should consider taking the steps necessary to lead a more balanced life. Chaos breeds chaos, after all. It only took Jimmy a few weeks of living in his chaotic new cycle before it began to change his personality and outlook entirely. For John, the chaos of driving to work has begun to encroach on every aspect of his life. For Julie, the yearning to justify every minute of the day has left her locked in a chaotic cycle from which there seems to be no escape. And for Jenny, an addiction to chaos has led to an addiction far more tangible.

If you have found yourself identifying with even one aspect of the lives of the Dawson family, then you are at risk for chaos addiction. But even if you are mired in an addiction already, it is not too late. The model that we have just outlined is like a key that will unlock the door to your chaos cycle. It will free you from your burden. And it will show you the way to a more balanced mode of living.

Now that you are aware of your own level of chaos and what the cycle of chaos looks like, we may move on to the ways you can make the Chaos Model work for you. In the chapters to come, you will learn how to spot the most chaotic areas in your life, how to develop a plan to break the cycle, and, ultimately, how to lead a more balanced life at home, in your marriage or relationship, with your children, and at work.

Chaos may be an addictive substance—and it may permeate almost every aspect of modern life—but that does not mean that there are no solutions to beating it. Read on to discover those solutions.

Chapter 8

Bringing It All Together

With the signs and components of chaos now fully defined, we may begin to construct ways for you to eliminate this destructive element. And if you take a look ahead, you will see that the coming chapters intend to apply a lesson in converting chaos to balance within four specific arenas of your daily life. Chaos at home, at work, with your children, and in your marriage can certainly be damaging. Fortunately, there is a true path to replacing that chaos with a more balanced approach to living.

But that balance isn't possible until we turn the search inward. With this chapter, we will begin to examine your own chaos picture. You will learn how to look for the warning signs of a chaos reaction. You will determine your own most threatening triggers. And you will begin to construct a plan to help bring balance into your daily routine.

When thinking about breaking free from the chaos cycle, a few important goals come to mind. Until these goals are achieved, it will be next to impossible to bring any measurable change into your life. The first goal is that you must accept that you may suffer from some form of chaos addiction—which has led or could lead to other addictions. Second, you must understand that your thinking contributes to your chaos addiction. And third, you must recognize the triggers that contribute to your potentially continuous lifestyle of destruction and self-sabotage.

In this chapter, you will learn some of the ways in which your negative thinking contributes to your addiction. You will also come to understand that your thinking may reflect a number of defense mechanisms such as denial or rationalization. You will be able to identify the difference between emotions and feelings, as well as find ways how to deal with them in your daily life.

In the end, you will come to realize exactly how the powerful and cunning problems of chaos addiction have affected your life. You will be better equipped to spot any existing old habits that have supported the cycles of chaos addiction. You will find the tools necessary to evaluate your current relationships, deciding whether or not they are healthy. And, ultimately, you will find the hope that you can overcome your addiction.

Later in the chapter, you will find a chaos workbook. This workbook offers a series of questions designed to get you thinking about the warning signs of chaos and how you manage them. But before we get down to answering those questions, we must address the information you will need in order to make calculated and honest answers.

Negative Thinking

Negative thinking is perhaps the most significant obstacle to balance. Consider your inner monologue the soundtrack of your life. If that soundtrack is constantly negative, your life is likely to follow suit. You will find yourself in bad situation after bad situation—all the while feeling trapped, as if no matter what you do, nothing changes. If your soundtrack is consistently positive, on the other hand, you will begin to see things in a different light. It will seem as if there is no such thing as a relationship that cannot be fixed, no routine that cannot be corrected or avoided.

The most substantial problem with negative thinking is that it tends to contribute to a resistance to change. This is because negative thinking is a natural defense mechanism designed to help the individual embrace the potential for (or fear of) failure. And the trouble with embracing failure and fear is that the act of doing so often generates more failure and fear than would otherwise be normal.

But how do you know if you are a negative thinker? Have you ever said anything like this: "It looks like a great day outside, but I know it's not going to last"? Negative thinkers have a tendency to find the downside to anything that would otherwise seem positive. If the sun is shining over the carefully planned picnic, the negative thinker tends to wait for (and even expect) rain.

On the surface, this might seem healthy. The negative thinker prepares him/herself for disaster before it even occurs. The trouble with this idea is that the act of waiting for the rain renders the negative thinker *unable to enjoy* the sun. The value of the afternoon picnic is lost because the negative thinker spends the entire time fretting about the "inevitable" poor ending. This could lead to a short temper, irritability, or standoffishness. And, figuratively speaking, that sort of thing would, of course, rain on everyone else's picnic.

To apply this idea more directly to the Chaos Model, a negative thinker is one who remains in the reaction state almost constantly. They receive triggers and feelings from their jobs, marriage, children, and routines and often react to them by complaining. In fact, a negative thinker complains almost constantly. He/she will claim the need for a new job, but then not do anything about it due to the fear of leaving his/her carefully constructed comfort zone. And that fear leads to more reactions, which lead to more negative situations and feelings, which lead to more negative thinking— and the whole cycle perpetuates itself.

Negative thinkers also tend to be excuse-makers. For example, not only will they complain about their job, but they will also make excuses for why it is the way it is. Instead of sending out résumés and applications, they explain that they can't afford to switch jobs now because they are too busy with their son's baseball team.

But even more damaging is the fact that negative thinking has a tendency to corrode relationships. Most people do not want to be around the kind of person who always looks for the bad in things, after all. How can someone enjoy the picnic if she has a friend who constantly reminds her that the picnic will soon end? Relationships are based on two or more people's desire to construct positive situations with one another— and negative thinkers have the tendency to impede that desire, given their penchant for dwelling on the negative in any given situation.

Feelings

Negative thinking is merely a way to address unfavorable emotions, the ultimate source of the feelings that can lead to chaotic behavior. So in order to understand why we might be subject to overly negative thinking, let's examine the emotions that serve as its root cause.

Anger

Anger amounts to losing the ability to think calmly about a given situation or event. So when you get angry, you are essentially giving up a part of your ability to think clearly and make proper decisions. Now, one common misconception about anger is that it is always destructive. This simply isn't true. There is such a thing as healthy anger. Everyone gets mad from time to time. It is what you do with the anger that creates problems.

Loneliness

For many people, this can be the most terrifying feeling one can encounter. This isolation, this disconnect from others, can leave people with the feeling that they are ultimately responsible for *everything* in life, however positive or negative.

Loneliness tends to perpetuate itself, as well. A person who feels lonely tends to be unwilling to utilize other people to create balance in his life. These kinds of people tend to drift around, feel sorry for themselves, and withdraw from social situations. Even when help is offered, they can't accept it, most often because they don't feel worthy of aid.

Sadness

We have all experienced sadness on certain levels. For many people, it can be a crippling feeling. It tends to lead to a flat, cheerless state. In addition, the sad individual often lacks motivation to make balanced decisions.

Reactions

As we have learned, the feelings derived from the emotions listed above tend to trigger specific reactions in the chaos addict. So let's take the next step in the model and break down the most common forms of reaction.

Denial

Denial is the act of ignoring or refusing to acknowledge a problem, regardless of how considerable it may be. It is the tendency to construct excuses for otherwise reckless behavior.

A person in denial often has difficulty changing any part of his routine, however negative that part may be. Alcoholics can't ever hope to put down the drink if they deny the possibility of their own alcoholism. In this sense, someone suffering from denial often creates the same triggers in his life, always reacting in the same way. Then, when those reactions lead to negative situations, he denies any complicity.

Projection

Projection is the act of blaming others for one's own misgivings. In other words, a person who projects does whatever she can to avoid responsibility for her actions. For example, if a woman suffering from projection blows up on her husband, she will most often say, "I'm sorry I yelled, honey, but you made me mad." In this case, the negative episode becomes the husband's fault, and any responsibility is dealt away. If there is a problem at school or work, this person will blame a teacher, coworker or boss. Her own reactions to given triggers/feelings are projected on to the other people in her life—thus, all responsibility for reacting negatively is assigned elsewhere.

Rationalization

Rationalization is essentially a fancy term for "making excuses." This defense mechanism allows people to view their own negative or unacceptable actions in a logical way. If one can rationalize a negative behavior, one does not have to deal with the truth about where it comes from. For example, one might rationalize an overly busy schedule by claiming that he is only happy when he feels productive. The only trouble with this line of thinking is that the rationalization helps one avoid the potential fact that he is not happy.

Intellectualization

People displaying intellectualization tend to spend most of their time within their own heads. Instead of looking at the grass roots of a problem, they attempt to examine things from an intellectual standpoint. In other words, intellectualization is the attempt to block all feelings or emotions with calculated thoughts. Intellectuals will remove themselves from any action or occurrence, however stressful, by retreating to the sanctity of their own minds.

Many people identify with these four defense mechanisms because when you break them all down, they all amount to reactions to help deal with responsibility. More importantly, they are all common symptoms of addiction. If you see yourself in any of these defense mechanisms, you likely have room to improve on your chaos to balance ratio.

The Six Habits of Highly Chaotic People

What if you have not yet found anything in this chapter with which to identify? Does that mean that you are not, in fact, addicted to chaos? Not necessarily. Admitting to anger and fear is difficult enough. Admitting to denial and rationalization is downright impossible. Fortunately, there are signs and symptoms of these feelings and reactions that are far easier to spot. Consider your habits. Do they include any of the following?

1. **Constant stress**
   Do you feel as if your work is never done? That the world is resting on your shoulders? Do you have difficulty relaxing or taking time off? Do you have trouble falling asleep at night because you can't stop thinking about all the things you have to remember to take care of? Then you might be suffering from too much stress.

2. **Consistent lateness**
   When was the last time you were on time for an appointment? For work? For a party? Showing up fashionably late might seem like a good thing to some, but if you can never seem to be on time, even when you try, then something else might be causing the issue. It isn't traffic. It isn't the kids. It isn't that you are overworked. It's that your life is too chaotic.

3. **Constant complaining**
   How often do you find yourself saying something positive? Do you complain about your job? About your marriage? About your children? About your social life? If you complain more often than you praise, something is driving you to a negative state.

4. **Being short on time**
   Do you feel like you never have enough time to do what you need to do? Do you feel rushed in everything, as if you're always running around like a chicken with its head cut off? Do you find it difficult to concentrate on one task because you are too busy thinking about all the other tasks you have yet to complete? If so, then you have most likely overbooked yourself. And as you have seen, overbooking and over scheduling can be symptoms of a chaos addiction.

5. **Over-analysis**
    Do you find that you have to justify your actions to other people? Do you make excuses for things like getting angry, being late, or failing to complete a task? Do you often have to defend the actions of your spouse, significant other, or friends? If so, you might be experiencing the kinds of reactions that lead directly to chaos.

6. **Regular arguments**
    Do you find that you always have to get the last word? Have you had one or more arguments with the people in your life today? Do you find yourself trying to convince people that your way of doing things is better than their way? Do you feel irritable on a regular basis? If so, there is something driving you to your anger. Something just beneath the surface could be causing you to go off on the people in your life.

Let us now move on to quantifying precisely the areas that have caused you the most trouble in the chaos cycle. Answer the questions in the workbook that follows as truthfully as possible, as your answers will help you to construct a Balance Plan—the plan that will finally deliver you from the seemingly endless cycle of chaos.

The Chaos Workbook

Ask yourself the following questions:

1. Am I happy with my life?
2. Am I the person I want to be?
3. Does it feel as if I am incapable of achieving personal growth or reaching my goals?
4. Do I feel that I am capable of reaching my potential or will I always have to settle for "second best"?
5. Am I unable to allow myself to feel happy and content?
6. Am I attracted to upheaval, chaos, or conflict?
7. Do I often find myself running around in circles, stuck, confused, or frustrated?
8. Do I purposely create turmoil for myself?
9. Do I find myself reacting to things or situations that I have no control over?
10. Am I struggling with other addictions (i.e., alcohol, drugs, sex, gambling)?
11. Am I attracted to illegal activities?
12. Have I done things that I could have been arrested for (or have I picked friends who have)?
13. Have I been involved in affairs, stolen from friends, or lied about something?
14. Have I ever spent money recklessly?
15. Have I ever lost my job, been sick a lot, or cost others money due to my recklessness/addictions?

Now, answer the following:

1. The changes I want to make are:

2. The most important reasons I want to make these changes are:

3. The steps I plan to take in changing are:

4. I will know that my plan is working if:

5. Some things that could interfere with my plan are:

Key Feelings
Loneliness, anxiety, anger, self-pity, grief, resentment

1. List the key feelings that you are having.

Character Defects
Jealousy, impulsiveness, greed, grandiosity, meanness, selfishness, arrogance

1. Which character defects do you have as a result of chaos addiction?

2.   How have these defects hurt others?

Assets

Generosity, love, heroism, kindness, sharing, charity, humility, compassion

1.   Make a list of your assets.

Instructions: Below are a number of events that individuals sometimes experience in relation to their chaos-addicted lifestyles. Read each one. Then list the number that indicates most accurately how often each has occurred within the past six months.

1.   Very much
2.   Somewhat
3.   Occasionally
4.   Never

Personalizing (   )
Thinking that all situations and events revolve around you. "Everyone was looking at me and wondering why I was there."

Magnifying (   )
Blowing negative events out of proportion. "This is the worst thing that could happen to me."

Minimizing (   )
Glossing over the positive factors. Overlooking the fact that nothing really bad happened. "It was nothing. Just a little fight, is all."

Either/or thinking ( )
Not taking the full picture into account. "Either I'm a loser or a winner."

Taking events out of context ( )
Fixating on one or two negative occurrences within an otherwise successful event. "I answered those two questions wrong; I blew the whole interview."

Jumping to conclusions ( )
Finding the extreme in even the most mundane details. "I have a swollen gland. This must be cancer."

Over-generalizing ( )
Taking one specific instance and applying it to the whole. "I always fail. I fail at everything I ever try."

Self-blame ( )
Always blaming oneself for everything. "I'm no good."

Magical thinking ( )
The assumption that you somehow deserve what life brings you. "Everything is bad because of the bad things that I've done in my past."

Mind reading ( )
Projecting your own insecurities into the minds of other people. "Everyone thought I was fat and ugly."

Comparing ( )
Comparing yourself to others. "She's so much prettier than me."

Catastrophe thinking ( )
Putting the worst possible outcome on events. "I just know something terrible is going to happen."

Control vs. No Control

Fortunately, even if the answers you have provided above point to a deep addiction to chaos, there are solutions. We move on now to determining the solutions that will work best for you.

We begin with the concept of control. The first step in any balanced life is to understand that no one has control over everything in life. No matter how hard you work, how hard you try, or how much you desire it, certain things simply lie outside your grasp. This is okay. As you will see, letting go of control over things that we cannot control actually leads to a greater sense of empowerment.

Keeping that in mind, let's take a quick look at feelings. The best and only way to deal with negative feelings is to identify the triggers that create them. In the case of anger, for example, you might find that your triggers are the people you associate with at work or at home. You might find that your job itself is a source of anger.

In a moment, you will be making a list of the triggers in your life that might lead to reactions. With this list, you will be able to begin constructing the picture of your own chaos cycle. But the first step toward breaking away from the cycle is to understand that there are certain triggers on your list that you will be able to control and certain triggers that you will have no control over. Acceptance is key. Know what you can change and learn to accept that which you cannot.

Take gas prices, for example. There is perhaps no greater hot-button issue in this country than what we pay at the pump. People complain constantly about gas prices: how unreasonable they are, how much it's costing them, etc. But why complain? Gas prices are not something that the average person can control. And no amount of complaining is going to bring back the days of the seventy-nine-cent gallon. Instead, when dealing with gasoline-related stress, we should be focusing on the things we *can* control. We can trade in our SUVs for economy cars. We can carpool. We can bike to work.

Of course, all of these things require sacrifice. We might have to go through the process of buying a new car. We might have to worry about dropping our car off at someone else's home so we can carpool. We might have to deal with sweat at the office. But if we do this—if we take control of the things we can control—we become empowered. We have squared off against the trigger known as gas prices and we have eliminated its power over our daily lives.

The bottom line is that you must focus on the things that you have control over and let go of the things that you don't. This might be a struggle for many people because letting go can be difficult. Many fear that by letting go, they will wind up spinning out of control—that without the comfort of the familiar, life will fall out of whack. It's funny, though; when we learn to let go of the things we cannot control, the opposite happens. We gain *more* control, *more* power over our lives.

The Four Triggers

There are four key areas in a person's life that tend to lead to triggers/feelings. With our how-to section on taking control of your triggers and seeking greater balance, we will address each of the following areas:

1. **Cognitive triggers**
   Cognitive triggers are those that exist within your own mind. Negative thinking is a cognitive trigger—and often contributes most significantly to a chaos addiction. These triggers may reflect a number of defense mechanisms such as denial or rationalization.

2. **Emotional triggers**
   It is easy to get caught up in the idea that emotions are equivalent to feelings. This is not true. Some examples of feelings are: anger, happiness, sadness, fear, and disgust. An emotion is simply the way in which we respond to our feelings. And even if feelings are unpredictable and sometimes difficult to manage, our emotions are something that we can control.

3. **Behavioral triggers**
   Behavioral triggers are perhaps the easiest to spot. They refer to the routines and habits in your life. You are likely to have many existing old habits that have supported the continuation of the cycle of chaos addiction.

4. **Social triggers**
   Social triggers may be the most painful to gain control over. They are spawned from the relationships in your life. Sometimes, taking control means coming to terms with the problems

in a given relationship. Sometimes, it may mean cutting the relationship off entirely.

Exercises

In addition to the Chaos Model, there are several key exercises that you may wish to work on in order to help break the cycle of chaos. Not every exercise fits every person, so be sure to read all the way through the list to see which among them would work best for you.

Record yourself

Keep a tape recorder in your pocket. For a full day, tape the conversations you have with family and friends. At the end of the day, listen to your words. Identify the common negative phrases that come up.

This may seem arbitrary, but it is actually quite powerful. The act of hearing how we speak is far more powerful than simply thinking about how we speak. Even if you feel that the way you think does not contribute to your chaos, you are likely to be startled at the level of your negativity.

Rewrite your histories

Another great exercise is known as cognitive reframing. Think about your most recent disastrous situation. It might have been an incident at work or an argument at home. Now, write down everything you remember about the situation. Write the story from beginning to end. Include how you felt and what you said or did.

Now, once you have this little narrative, go through and edit it. Change all the negative phrases to positive ones. When you have finished, you should have a story that reads in an entirely different way. This demonstrates the vast difference between positive and negative thinking, as well as the insignificant changes that you will need to make to significantly reframe your line of thinking.

Schedule for relaxation

Take a look at your schedule. How many hours in a given week have you left open for leisure activities? None? Then it is time to create a leisure plan. If you plan every minute of your working day, then you should also work to plan every minute of your leisure time. And do what you can to make the two elements balance. For every three hours of obligation, you should schedule an hour of leisure. Take time to read, relax, exercise, and just generally have fun.

Keep a journal

Many people addicted to chaos find themselves in so many chaotic situations that they are often difficult to keep straight. How can you quantify the many problematic occurrences in your life if you're constantly engaged in problematic situations? Keeping a journal of your daily activities is a good start.

When you see your actions narrated on paper, it is far easier to understand how they can be negative and potentially damaging. Sometimes, keeping everything in our own heads can make things more complicated than they actually are. Writing things down eliminates that problem. Journaling your life will make balancing it out a whole lot easier.

Write down your reactions to certain events. Jot down every negative thought. And be honest with yourself.

The Balance Plan

The Balance Plan lies on the exact opposite pole from the chaos cycle. With your Chaos Model, you now have an understanding of your triggers/feelings, your reactions, and a series of decisions that might help alleviate chaos. Now that you have all of those tools in place, you may use them to construct a specific plan toward a more balanced way of living. Keep to your Balance Plan and you will be able to avoid chaos in the future—and the only sure way to conquer addiction is to consistently avoid those situations that fed the addiction in the first place.

In the chapters to come, you will learn how to apply the Balance Plan to the four major arenas of life: home, parenting, marriage (or other relationships), and work. But before we may do that, we must outline how, exactly, to create your own.

The approach has eight steps:

1. List your triggers.
2, Break your triggers into two lists—one list being those triggers that you may control and the other being those that you may not.
3. Identify how each trigger makes you feel (one trigger may create fear, for example, while another may generate anger).
4. Identify what each of these feelings means to you.
5. Determine the reactions these feelings lead to.
6. Develop a decision tree—a list of all the things you could do to make a decision rather than to react to your list of triggers (and be sure to write all of this down).

7. Outline the situations in your life that most commonly lead to chaos.
8. Use the Chaos Model as a guide.

This final point is an important one. With all of your triggers, feelings, and chaotic situations at hand, you may now take a look at the model and plug each point into its respective box. For example, if one of your chaotic situations involved your boss telling you that you weren't working hard enough, then your feeling of anger would be placed in the Triggers/Feelings box. Then, in the Reaction box, you might write that you actually did the opposite of what your boss told you, just to spite her. In the corresponding Decision box, you would list a more positive reaction (such as, "Call a meeting with my boss to discuss how I might improve my productivity").

Controlling Your Triggers
With the Balance Plan on paper, we may turn focus toward applying it to our daily lives. The plan will help you to determine the steps to eliminating or otherwise minimizing the effects of the following triggers.

Cognitive Triggers

Step One: Focus on the here and now.

Many people aren't able to enjoy the moment because they are always thinking about tomorrow or next month or next year. So the first step toward balance and control is a matter of breaking an old habit. Concentrate on what you are doing right now, not what you have to do later.

Step Two: Accept responsibility for your own actions.

It is so easy to blame others for our own misgivings. It is easier still to make excuses for our behaviors. Not until we recognize that we are responsible for the things we choose to do and say may we break the cycle of chaos.

Step Three: Keep it simple.
We all do it from time to time: overanalyze situations. Life is as complicated or as simple as we make it. Where possible, work to simplify.

Step Four: Look for the things you can change.

In the Control vs. No Control section, you learned that there are many things in life that simply can't be controlled. Focus only on that which you can control and you will come to accept that which you cannot.

Emotional Triggers

Step One: Make a list of "I" messages.

This step is most useful for those suffering from reactions to anger (reactions like projection). Sit down and make a list of phrases that begin with the word "I." For example, "I want," "I need," "I feel," etc. If you come to embrace these kinds of action phrases in your life, you will gradually eliminate your tendency to blame others for your own mistakes.

Step Two: Make a list of your triggers.

If traffic triggers feelings of anger, include it in the list. If your children trigger unfavorable reactions, write them down as well. The goal here is to create as thorough and comprehensive a list as possible. If you can see your triggers on paper, they become tangible and far easier to control.

Step Three: Determine which triggers can and which triggers cannot be controlled.

This point has been alluded to already. You now have a list in front of you, but you must understand (and embrace the fact) that you can't control every point. Highlight the ones that you can control. Come to terms with the ones that you can't.

Behavioral Triggers

Step One: Be conscious of your body language and tone of voice.

Your own demeanor can trigger unfavorable reactions in others. In this way, the manner in which you carry yourself can dictate (or at least influence) the frequency and level of your chaos. If you look and sound like you are ready for an argument, the people around you are far more likely to start one.

Step Two: Determine the situations you are in that create negative reactions.

Everyone suffering from chaos addiction has at least one environment in which their chaos is perpetuated. Many times, we have come to rationalize our behaviors or tendencies to fall back into these environments. "I have to drive in gridlock because I have to get to my job." This is not an acceptable statement. Make a list of all those places or circumstances that make you feel stressed, angry, or afraid. Once you become aware of these problematic situations, you can work toward breaking those patterns.

Step Three: Avoid those situations.

Simple enough. Once you have your list of unfavorable circumstances, you may now take steps to avoid them.

Social Triggers

Step One: Avoid isolation.

Keeping to yourself has many potentially negative side effects. For one, it leads to strain on existing relationships, as people tend to feel slighted by a person's apparent desire to avoid them. For another, time alone represents time for negative self-talk. It is easier to fall into a pattern of negativity if there is no one around to refute the negative thinking.

Step Two: Avoid people who are negative or attempt to "push your buttons."

Just as our own minds can become damaging, so, too, can the opinions of negative people. If you surround yourself with people who constantly cut you down or tell you that you can't do something you know you can do, it is only a matter of time before your self-talk starts to align with their negative statements. Most people addicted to chaos have at least one of these people in their lives. Once you have identified them, work to change the relationship or avoid it altogether.

Step Three: Create a support network.

Just as you are likely to have people in your life who influence you in a negative way, you are sure to have people in your life who influence you in a positive way. Determine who these people are, then plan to spend more time with them. Positive people tend to reinforce positive thinking. Whether it is a weekly visit or a daily phone call, your support network can work wonders on your levels of chaos. Networks such as these have the added bonus of creating a sense of belonging and control, which tends to eliminate most fears.

Conclusion

In this chapter, we have done little more than scratch the surface. Coupled with the Chaos Model, the Balance Plan is truly a powerful tool to overcoming chaos addiction. But the potential for chaos lies everywhere—often in places we least expect. Read on to discover exactly how to apply the plan at home, with your children, in your marriage, and at work.

Chapter 9

Chaos at Home

We move on now to apply what you have learned about chaos and balance to a few circumstances and situations quite common in daily life. In the coming chapters, we will explore chaos in marriage, in parenting, and at work. But no study on how to eliminate chaos can begin without a thorough examination of chaos within the environment in which we all spend the majority of our time: the home.

A word on the chaos cycle before we delve into the arena in which it thrives: Chaos may be generated by everyday triggers and feelings but nothing compounds it more than the relationships we choose to maintain. Simply put, healthy relationships create balance while unhealthy ones create chaos.

Given that point, what makes for a healthy relationship? How can we know when the relationships in our lives are beneficial and positive?

The characteristics of a healthy relationship include:

- Open communication without either party feeling the need to become defensive or moody

- No interruption during communication (each person always waits for his/her turn to speak)
- Acceptance of the other's feelings
- The readiness of each party to take responsibility for his/her own behavior
- A willingness to change
- A willingness to work through and solve problems
- A willingness to compromise
- Cooperative decision-making
- The ability to disagree without getting angry or frustrated
- The ability for each party to see themselves in the other's shoes

Healthy relationships, for the chaos addict, might seem rather rare. For good reason: Chaos addicts often surround themselves with unhealthy relationships, as unhealthy relationships are often the cause as well as the effect of chaos addiction. So how do you know if a relationship in your life is unhealthy?

You might experience any of the following:

- Dishonesty
- Blaming
- Lying
- Arguing
- Unfaithfulness
- Stress
- Defensiveness
- Anger
- Overreaction
- Noncooperation
- Lack of compromise

Each of the points above contributes greatly to one's level of chaos. The more often a person encounters these particular triggers, the more chaos one might expect in life.

Fortunately, an unhealthy relationship may be fixed. It may be converted into a healthy relationship so long as both parties are willing to make some changes themselves. A significant part of this process is for you to begin to identify the triggers that create the problems in the relationship. Once you have identified the triggers, you may begin to look for solutions—you may begin to determine the decisions (and not the reactions) that will contribute to making the relationship healthier.

One must have the tools to look at one's own behaviors, and this is exactly where the Balance Plan and the Chaos Model come into play. Denial, anger, and a need to blame the other person may be overcome if these two strategies are properly applied.

But there is something else to keep in mind, as well. No matter how willing you might be to change, there may be certain relationships in your life that cannot be fixed. Occasionally, you will encounter people completely incapable of change—whether due to their own chaos or other presenting addictions. You may find coworkers at your job who just can't seem to smooth things over. There may be people in your social or family life too addicted to drugs or alcohol to control their behavior. You may encounter individuals too unethical to seek change in themselves. In these cases, the only solution is to take the steps necessary to remove these relationships from your life.

Leaving these damaging relationships can be frightening. Change of any kind can be scary, particularly if it involves people we love or care about. But if you are to beat your chaos addiction, you must occasionally make difficult sacrifices. You must do what you can to break away from the safety of your structure and the comfort of your routine. Unhealthy relationships contribute directly to unhealthy routines. They also have the tendency to mask one's own feelings of inadequacy or fear of change.

Financial Burden

In the hope of finding solutions for the most commonly unhealthy relationships, let us examine a few traditional contributors to chaos in the home. We begin with something almost all of us can identify with: financial burden.

Imagine that you have just gotten the latest statement for your joint checking account with your spouse or significant other. Your eyes flit to the most important number first: the balance. Your heart skips as you realize that the number is far smaller than you anticipated.

So you begin to pour over the numbers, itemizing each purchase and deposit for the month. Several purchases jump out at you. An expensive pair of shoes. A bar tab for a bar you don't remember visiting. Several parking charges at a ramp in a part of town you rarely visit. Tickets for an upcoming show, one that you don't recall being invited to. Now, these purchases jump out at you because you know you didn't collaborate on them with your spouse or significant other. He/she never got the "okay" from you. Not that you lord over the decisions regarding spending—it's just that the two of you usually confirm luxury purchases before swiping the card or cutting the check.

Now, as you look over the bill, there are a few potential triggers/feelings that you may encounter.

So let's begin by examining Box 1 of the Chaos Model:

Box 1: Triggers/Feelings
Triggers:
- A lower than expected checking account balance
- The suspicion that your spouse/significant other is responsible for the lower balance

Potential Feelings:
- Anger
- Frustration
- Fear (that bills won't be paid)
- Jealousy (he/she had all the fun that you can't have now that the budget is exhausted)

Note that each of these points is a feeling, not an emotion. You may still feel all of them, even though you continue to love your spouse/significant other. You may also maintain your emotions for the other people in your life that your reactions might affect.

So in the hopes of avoiding such a situation and moving toward balance, let's turn our attention now to Box 2 of the model:

Box 2: Decision
Potential Decisions:
- Plan to meet with your spouse/significant other in private (away from children, family, friends, or coworkers).

> - Calmly discuss with your spouse/significant other why they made the purchases without asking (do not yell, accuse, point fingers, or harass).
> - Remind your spouse/significant other that bills still need to be paid and that his/her impulse spending might put you in a tight spot at the end of the month.
> - Reach a mutual resolution to the problem in the hopes of ensuring that it will not happen again.

Unfortunately, for people suffering from chaos addiction, the actions above aren't often the first that come to mind. Instead, they tend to live in the reaction end of the spectrum.

Let's examine, then, Box 3 of the model:

Box 3: Reactions

Potential Reactions:

- Yell at spouse/significant other the moment he/she walks through the door.
- Hold the conversation (or argument) in public, in front of children, family, coworkers, or friends.
- Blame the spouse/significant other for his/her misdeeds.
- Fail to listen to any explanation, regardless of how logical or justified that explanation may be.
- Guilt the spouse/significant other ("Well, if you hadn't bought those shoes, we might have been able to go to the movies tonight").
- React to other situations with more anger than would be normal.

It's so easy to take the road described by the reactions listed above. This is the main reason that so many of us lead lives of constant chaos. That chaos, in turn, can compound any number of other triggers/feelings in your life, and the whole ugly cycle builds upon itself.

Let's examine now the chaos that such reactions might generate:

> **Box 4: Chaos**
> *Potential Chaos:*
> - Loss of focus (on work, relaxation, obligations, etc.) due to anger or frustration
> - The degradation of the relationship
> - The potential end of the relationship (people can say some truly nasty things when they are jealous or angry)
> - Sleeping on the couch (which might lead to loss of sleep, which leads to any number of other problems)
> - Driving the spouse/significant other to continue the behavior (just to spite you)

Chaos is a complicated matter. The list above isn't even close to complete. Social strife has the potential to go in any number of directions, none of them favorable. And all of them lead to more chaos.

Traffic

Let's now turn our attention to examining another common situation with the potential to generate chaos in the home. As you have seen, many people tend to construct schedules for themselves that leave them far too busy. The chaos addict might find him/herself over-committing to things to the point of absurdity.

But what happens when he/she is scheduled to have only five minutes of commute time to get to an obligation thirty miles away?

> **Box 1: Triggers/Feelings**
> *Triggers:*
> - An overly full daily schedule
> - The need to get to an important commitment in less time than is feasible
>
> *Potential Feelings:*
> - Anxiousness
> - Frustration
> - Self-loathing
> - Helplessness

Just about everyone can relate to this range of emotions. There is perhaps nothing more stressful than knowing you need to be somewhere and having no means to get there. These are always the situations when it seems that every stoplight is red, traffic is backed up, and everyone's driving slowly.

The reactions might seem obvious, but the decisions are certainly more effective.

> **Box 2: Decisions**
> *Potential Decisions:*
> - Accept that there is nothing you can do to get to your obligation on time.
> - Call ahead to explain that you will be late.
> - Listen to soothing music.

Traffic can be infuriating. Being late can be frustrating. But you have to accept that there is literally nothing that you can do about it.

Certainly, the reactions that follow do not help:

> **Box 3: Reactions**
> *Potential Reactions:*
> - Yelling at traffic, stoplights, slow drivers, etc.
> - Laying on the horn
> - Driving aggressively
> - Cursing yourself

Not only do the above reactions have a tendency to heighten chaos and stress rather than alleviate it, they also tend to breed chaos in other drivers.

Consider the following chaotic situations:

> **Box 4: Chaos**
> *Potential Chaos:*
> - Slower traffic
> - Car accidents

> - Heightened anger
> - More time passes, making you later than you would have
>   been otherwise

Traffic is perhaps the most visual representation of the evidence that reactions tend to make chaos worse. The natural reaction in traffic is to scream and yell and drive aggressively, which causes everything to slow down.

Oversleeping

Another common chaotic situation happens in the morning in many households, particularly when those houses are occupied by several children. For many parents, getting all the children up and ready for school in the morning is a constant struggle. It gets especially difficult when the parents themselves wake up late.

Imagine that, normally, you and your spouse/significant other each set an alarm, since you wake up at separate times in the morning. But overnight, there was a storm, knocking out your power and resetting your alarm clocks. By the time you wake up, you realize from your wristwatch that it is twenty after seven. You know you have less than a half-hour to get ready if you're going to make it to work on time. This wouldn't be a problem if you were on your own. But you have to give your spouse/significant other time to get ready. And then there are the children to think about. They need at least ninety minutes on the best of days.

You look over and see that your spouse/significant other is still sleeping soundly. A wave of panic washes over you.

A host of other triggers/feelings might follow:

Box 1: Triggers/Feelings
Triggers:
- Alarm clock doesn't go off
- The danger of being terribly late for work

Potential Feelings:
- Anger
- Frustration

> - Fear
> - Anxiety

Anger and frustration are obvious reactions. It's so easy to get angry at the fact that your alarm clock is blinking 12:00, even though it might seem absurd when thinking about the idea of getting angry at a storm. Storms are not something that we can control, and yet we react and blame them for our own problems. Fear is a more complicated issue, though it comes from an honest place. When we have little time to get things done, we tend to fear getting into fights: with a spouse/significant other, with the children, with the boss at work, etc. For whatever reason, we occasionally want to blame our spouse/significant other for not waking up earlier— even though he/she had no more control over the situation than we did—and that almost always leads to an epic argument. And then top it off with the anxiety that comes with knowing you will have to complete something that usually takes thirty minutes in less than half the time.

Despite all this, there are plenty of reasonable decisions to make:

Box 2: Decisions
Potential Decision:
- Calmly wake your spouse/significant other and explain the situation.
- Offer to skip your shower and help move the kids along.
- Make a quick breakfast.
- Politely ask your children to hurry as much as possible.
- Call ahead to work to explain that you might be late.

These decisions serve several purposes. First, they have the potential to speed up the morning routine, thereby making up for lost time. Second, they keep everyone in the family calm and focused on the task at hand (getting ready as quickly as possible). And third, it lets your employer know that you might be later than usual, but that you are willing to take the initiative and responsibility for the issue.

But, unfortunately, when we have our backs to the wall regarding social or professional obligations, so many of us tend to spend all of our time in the reaction state. How could we blame ourselves? Given the lack of time at hand, it becomes far more difficult to take the time to reason things out.

Box 3: Reactions
Potential Reactions:
- Yelling at spouse/significant other, children, coworkers, etc.
- Forcing everyone to skip a part of their daily routine (a shower, breakfast, working out, finishing homework, etc.)
- Rushing through everything
- Driving aggressively to work

All of these reactions can obviously be damaging. But there's another thing they have in common: None of them actually solves the problem at hand. In fact, they have a tendency to make matters far worse. Chaos will compound the problem every time.

Box 4: Chaos
Potential Chaos:
- Arguments
- Distractions
- Resentment
- The slowdown of the morning routine
- Traffic-related chaos

Obviously, when one reacts by yelling, arguments tend to break out. And the more time you spend arguing with your spouse/significant other and/or children, the later you will become. All that time spent arguing could have been better spent on taking care of the typical morning obligations. If the arguing had not occurred, you might have had time to serve your children a proper breakfast. And if they hadn't started their day off in the arguing mindset, they might not have spent all morning yelling at each other—and, in turn, might have had time to actually eat that proper breakfast. And in all cases, the cycle of resentment could have been avoided. The resentment of the alarm clock; the resentment of the spouse/significant other for not having greater control over the alarm clock; the resentment of the children for not hurrying when told to hurry; the resentment on the part of the children for being barked at all morning; the resentment of having to dress quickly; the resentment of having to go hungry to work/school; the resentment of traffic for not understanding that you are in a rush; the resentment of everyone at work/school for not appreciating your harried attitude—all can be avoided by taking that extra moment to reason things out and make a decision, one that leads to greater balance for your hasty morning routine.

Balancing the Home

Let's now examine each of the above three scenarios together and create a Balance Plan that will help to eliminate the chaos associated with each. This will begin to give you an idea about the kinds of things you might do to eliminate chaos in your own home. If you can find solutions to these three most common sources of chaos, then you can find solutions to any source that might be found at home.

Step One: List your triggers.

For the three scenarios highlighted above, the triggers are as follows:

- A lower than expected checking account balance
- The suspicion that your spouse/significant other is responsible for the lower balance
- An overly full daily schedule
- The need to get to an important commitment in less time than is feasible
- Alarm clock doesn't go off
- The danger of being terribly late for work

Step Two: Break your triggers into two lists—one list being those triggers that you may control and the other being those that you may not.

The above list was created as it was for good reason: It is perfectly symmetrical. If you look at the six points and think them through, it becomes clear that there are three that one can control and three that one cannot. Let's begin with the ones that can be controlled:

• A lower than expected checking account balance

It is important to note that past transgressions cannot be controlled. No matter how much yelling you do with your spouse/significant other or the bank, you won't get that money back. If you keep a level head while having the discussion about the balance with your spouse/significant other, however, two things are far more likely occur. First, your spouse/significant other might see the error of his/her ways and offer to return the unapproved purchases. Second, your spouse/significant other will think twice about repeating the mistake in the future.

• An overly full daily schedule

As you have seen with the story of the Dawsons, an overly full daily schedule is something that can easily be controlled. One simply has to make sacrifices. Understand that you cannot be responsible for everything, that people need time to relax in order to have balance in their lives, and that it is completely impossible to be in two places at once. Do this and your overly busy schedule takes care of itself.

• The alarm clock doesn't go off.

This one is tricky because it has one element that can be controlled and one element that cannot. You cannot control the fact that the storm reset your alarm, but you can take steps to ensure that it never happens again. Consider purchasing an alarm clock that runs on battery power as a backup. Or consider using your cell phone instead of an alarm. Most cell phones have alarm features, and storms can't reset their functionality.

Now, on to the points that you cannot control.

• The suspicion that your spouse/significant other is responsible for the lower balance

It's so easy to point fingers when a cause for concern presents itself. And when presented with a list of purchases that we don't remember, it is extremely difficult to avoid the reaction of suspicion. Suspecting the spouse/significant other is natural. It's how we react to that suspicion that matters.

• The need to get to an important commitment in less time than is feasible

If the drive to the commitment takes thirty minutes on Monday, it will take thirty minutes on Friday. There is no justifying the idea that we might be able to cut time off the commute if we drive faster, take a different route, or go at a different time (to avoid traffic). Such measures cannot be relied upon to deliver any significant improvement in drive time. So we cannot control how long it takes us to get somewhere. We can, however, control how long we allow ourselves to get there.

• The danger of being terribly late for work

Once circumstances have left us late for work, there is nothing we can do about it. We are simply going to be late. But one thing that can be done to help alleviate the consequences of being late is to call ahead and explain the situation. This shows initiative and thoughtfulness. And it takes a situation that we cannot control and makes it all the less chaotic.

Step Three: Identify how each trigger makes you feel.

In the above three Chaos Model exercises, we have already outlined a few of the feelings we might experience, given the circumstances.

> • Anger
> • Frustration
> • Fear
> • Jealousy
> • Anxiousness
> • Self-loathing
> • Helplessness

Step Four: Identify what each of these feelings means to you.

For each person, these feelings can mean different things. Take the time to list what each of them means to you.

- Anger:
- Fear:
- Jealousy:
- Anxiousness:
- Self-loathing:
- Helplessness:

Step Five: Determine the reactions these feelings lead to.

Our Chaos Models above have already led us to these reactions, as well. Take note of them again, however, as they are remarkably common.

If you see yourself in any of them, this Balance Plan will certainly help in your own life.

- Yell at spouse/significant other the moment he/she walks through the door.
- Hold the conversation (or argument) in public, in front of children, family, coworkers, or friends.
- Blame the spouse/significant other for his/her misdeeds.
- Fail to listen to any explanation, regardless of how logical or justified that explanation may be.
- Guilt the spouse/significant other ("Well, if you hadn't bought those shoes, we might have been able to go to the movies tonight").
- React to other situations with more anger than would be normal.
- Yell at traffic, stoplights, slow drivers, etc.
- Lay on the horn.
- Drive aggressively.
- Curse yourself.
- Yell at spouse/significant other, children, coworkers, etc.
- Force everyone to skip a part of their daily routine (a shower, breakfast, working out, finishing homework, etc.).

> - Rush through everything.
> - Drive aggressively to work.

Step Six: Develop a decision tree—a list of all the things you could do to make a decision rather than react to your list of triggers.

With our Chaos Model, we have already begun to construct a list of short-term decisions that could be made to help lessen chaos. But there are long-term decisions that could certainly help, as well.

First, the short-term decisions:

> - Plan to meet with your spouse/significant other in private (away from children, family, friends, or coworkers).
> - Calmly discuss with your spouse/significant other why they made the purchases without asking (do not yell, accuse, point fingers, or harass).
> - Remind your spouse/significant other that bills still need to be paid and that his/her impulse spending might put you in a tight spot at the end of the month.
> - Reach a mutual resolution to the problem in the hopes of ensuring that it will not happen again.
> - Accept that there is nothing you can do to get to your obligation on time.
> - Call ahead to work to explain that you will be late.
> - Listen to soothing music.
> - Calmly wake your spouse/significant other and explain the situation.
> - Offer to skip your shower and help move the kids along.
> - Make a quick breakfast.
> - Politely ask your children to hurry as much as possible.

It is easy to see that the above list carries the potential to alleviate stress and even eliminate chaos. But there are also long-term decisions that we might embrace as we move forward—decisions that will help remove the need to make almost all of these short-term decisions in the future and that will help to avoid the triggers that create our potentially problematic feelings in the first place.

To reduce stress with the family:

• Create a division of labor chart

A chart that divides chores and obligations among everyone in the family has so many benefits that lead to balance. First, it ensures that all work done around the house actually gets done. Second, it gives everyone equal responsibility for the upkeep of the home. And third, it makes everything run smoothly (and far more quickly) in the event that the family is late. Those mornings after a reset alarm are certainly more harmonious if everyone wakes knowing what they have to do.

• Develop social boundaries

Sometimes, we feel like we need to have our hand in everything. Our perceived need to control can lead us to encroach on the other members of our family—into their private lives and even their private space. If the family takes the time to reason out where the lines need to be drawn, the need to control tends to evaporate. It is strange how giving up control can be so empowering. But do this with your family and you will find its bonds tightening, strengthening, and working more harmoniously.

• Allow yourself to schedule some free time.

We have already covered the problem with over scheduling at length. When drawing up your schedule, it is important to remember that free time is every bit as necessary as busy time. For every three hours of work and/or obligation, consider scheduling at least an hour of leisure.

• Make a daily list of goals.

This list should include only three things that you want to accomplish each day. Make sure that they are reasonable and attainable. Your goal cannot be to get a new job by lunchtime or land on the moon before dinner. Make them small, but important. Consider things like "Get to work on time," or "Finish that expense report," or "Make a healthy dinner for the kids." This list has a couple of benefits. First, it keeps you motivated as the day goes on. And second, it reminds you at the end of the day that you have accomplished something. Too often, people think that they haven't accomplished anything with their days—even when they are constantly busy and getting things done all the time. Having a list to examine (and cross things off of) is a visual representation of your own productivity. But, again, remember to keep it simple. You can't have a list thirty points long (and full of unreasonable tasks).

- Eliminate clutter.

The space we live and work in has all kinds of potential to generate chaos. Misplacing something can be frustrating. When this sort of thing happens, we tend to blame others as much as we blame ourselves. Take steps to become more organized. Create an organizational chart, file things away, get rid of old junk, and take steps to prevent yourself from getting too cluttered in the future. Do this at home and you will find your family life to be more harmonious. Do this at work and you will never again have to stress about missing a deadline because you have misplaced something.

- Take stress breaks.

When we get stressed or anxious, it is easy to fall into the trap of feeling like we have to solve all of our problems in the moment, as soon as possible. This simply isn't true. Problems can wait. And they are better solved with a level head. So whenever you are feeling stressed, be sure to take stress breaks. Take a five-minute walk. Listen to your favorite soothing song from beginning to end. Take a quick drive (preferably in a traffic-clear area). Just generally get away from the situation. Then, when you have had some time to cool down, return to the problem that caused the stress and sort it out.

All of these solutions have the power to drastically reduce chaos in the future. But they take some dedication on your part. Incorporate them into your life—and stick to them—and you will find yourself living in a far more balanced way.

Step Seven: Outline the situations in your life that most commonly lead to chaos.

Step Seven, in this case, is open for you to complete. Now that you have seen a few of the situations that most commonly lead to chaos in the home, it is time for you to consider your own. What problems do you find yourself dealing with most often at home? When do you feel the most stressed? What causes you to fall back into the behaviors that lead to more chaos in your life?

Try to come up with five situations that you most often encounter. Then, with Step Eight, you will begin to look at and fill out your own Chaos Model.

Chaos Scenarios:

1.
2.
3.
4.
5.

Step Eight: Use the Chaos Model as a guide.

Now, using the following model, list all of your chaos scenarios, then the feelings associated with them, followed by decisions, reactions, and chaos. Having a visual aid such as this one will greatly help you in eliminating chaos and avoiding or solving the problems that generate it.

Scenario 1:

Box 1: Triggers/Feelings
Triggers:
-
-
-

Potential Feelings:
-
-
-
-
-

Box 2: Decisions
Potential Decisions:
-
-
-
-
-

Box 3: Reactions
Potential Reactions:
-
-
-
-
-

Box 4: Chaos
Potential Chaos:
-
-
-
-
-

Scenario 2:

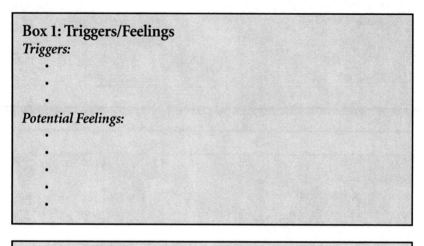

Box 1: Triggers/Feelings
Triggers:
-
-
-

Potential Feelings:
-
-
-
-
-

Box 2: Decisions
Potential Decisions:
-
-
-
-
-

Box 3: Reactions
Potential Reactions:
-
-
-
-
-

Box 4: Chaos
Potential Chaos:
-
-
-
-
-

Scenario 3:

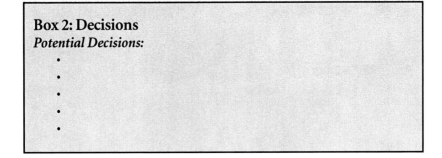

Box 1: Triggers/Feelings
Triggers:
-
-
-

Potential Feelings:
-
-
-
-
-

Box 2: Decisions
Potential Decisions:
-
-
-
-

Box 3: Reactions
Potential Reactions:
-
-
-
-
-

Box 4: Chaos
Potential Chaos:
-
-
-
-
-

Scenario 4:

Box 1: Triggers/Feelings
Triggers:
-
-
-

Potential Feelings:
-
-
-
-
-

Box 2: Decisions
Potential Decisions:
-
-
-
-
-

Box 3: Reactions
Potential Reactions:
-
-
-
-
-

Box 4: Chaos
Potential Chaos:
-
-
-
-
-

Scenario 5:

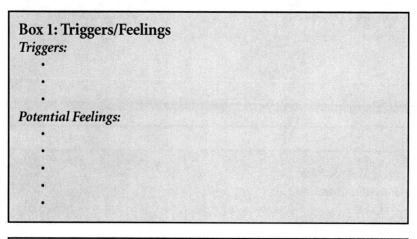

Box 1: Triggers/Feelings
Triggers:
-
-
-

Potential Feelings:
-
-
-
-
-

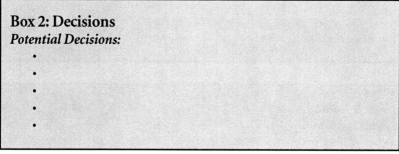

Box 2: Decisions
Potential Decisions:
-
-
-
-
-

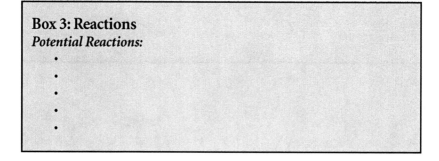

Box 3: Reactions
Potential Reactions:
-
-
-
-
-

Box 4: Chaos
Potential Chaos:
-
-
-
-
-

Chapter 10

Childhood
and Parenting Chaos

The parent/child relationship is just like any other, except that it is perhaps a bit more sensitive and complex than most. Parents and children tend to experience chaos in their relationships every day. This increase in frequency of chaos is likely due to the fact that while children and parents go through their own independent chaos, they are also heavily dependent on one another. In most healthy families, when a parent experiences something, so, too, does the child, and vice versa.

In this sense, both parties are the victims as well as the instigators of chaos. This chaos is most often caused by triggers such as blame, dishonesty, and frustration. Anger and overreaction are never too far behind.

But regardless of the source of chaos, it is the parent who holds the key to breaking the cycle. How a parent reacts to his/her child can make all the difference in how the relationship grows and evolves.

For example, imagine a parent who blames his child for a messy household. While the parent is the authority figure and has the right to lay down the rules, the reaction of the child is too often overlooked. The child, in fact, frequently returns the blame to the parent for being what he or she interprets as cruel or unfair. This goes unnoticed because a child is rarely as vocal about his/her feelings as the parent. Either that or the parent tends to refuse to listen.

The same goes for when a parent catches a child lying, or simply accuses him of it. If a parent doesn't understand a child's reason for lying (most often as a way to avoid punishment), a lack of trust may cause a further breakdown of communication. But a lie can't go unnoticed or unpunished. Parents and children have to find a balance.

Whatever the situation, the relationship calls for a willingness to change, to cooperate, and to develop. But as is typical in relationships in the home, certain situations that spark chaos, whether expected or not, will undoubtedly occur. Consider the following examples as a basis for our examination of chaos in the parent/child relationship.

Homework/Schooling

Parents and children interact on many different levels. While many of these levels are complex in nature, the interaction during the child's school days is perhaps the most complex. At the very least, it is often a breeding ground for chaos. School is an exciting chapter in both a parent and child's life, but given that the child now spends so many hours per day being physically distant from home, it can lead to a sincere struggle in the relationship.

Homework in this country has arguably gotten out of control. Each year, it seems that more and more children are expected to complete more and more work at home on a nightly basis. This increased workload had led to arguably the most significant cause of stress between children and their parents.

But the volume of assignments isn't the only reason for school-related chaos; kids today are busier than seems reasonable. They experience more parental-pressure and peer-pressure to be successful than ever before. Success isn't just measured by the number of A's a student receives; it is also measured by the number of activities in which they participate. Children have to learn to balance basketball with algebra, student council with history, and biology with ballet—a task just as difficult, if not more difficult, than passing an exam.

These extracurricular activities, coupled with the increase in the amount of homework, not only cause stress to the child, but create a tremendous amount of strain on the parent/child relationship, as well. While children flail to balance all their activities with their homework, the parents are right there making sure it all gets done. This can lead to the "slave-driver" effect, which breeds resentment in most children.

With all that said, it's important to note that the child's busy schedule is not all that we must blame. Many parents find themselves equally busy with their jobs, their housework, their hobbies, and their social lives. The parents might work more than one job, have an odd shift, or submit to extended or inconsistent hours. On top of all that, a parent still has to be a parent.

Add to this the pressure to get into college placed on the child at an ever younger age. Today, if you ask children what they want to be when they grow up, you might be surprised to discover that their goals are very high. Many children, even before middle school, have dreams of being a doctor, lawyer, or scientist, and they know exactly how they are going to get there.

Perhaps the children have set healthy, attainable goals for themselves (or perhaps the parents have done it for them), but straight A's, exceptional test scores, maximum social involvement, and acceptance into a top-tier university might be asking too much. Not *every* child can live up to such high expectations.

So can a parent blame a child for struggling academically? After all the chaos of everyday life and the pressure for success, very few people would have the time, the energy, and the patience remaining for homework or the extra stresses involved with school and furthering education. With all this pressure mounting, it is no wonder that completing the nightly assignment slides down the ladder of priorities. It is no wonder that just getting a child through the homework is a struggle unto itself. But the more the homework chaos compounds, the less the child will care for school. With that decline in care, the desire to further education and attain goals is sure to decline right along with it. Because of his overworked schedule, the student might begin to fail. And with failure comes more chaos.

With the family overbooked and the kids stuck in the middle, there are certainly many potential triggers to watch out for.

So let's take another look at the Chaos Model when applied to childhood and parenting chaos during a child's school days:

Box 1: Triggers/Feelings
Triggers:
- The child fails an exam.
- The child is overbooked or cannot manage his priorities.

Potential Feelings:
- Concern
- Frustration

- Fear (that your child isn't succeeding or is depressed)
- Mistrust
- Anger

No matter how much you trust your child to complete his/her work or how involved you are in his/her daily activities, failure is always a part of life. And that failure will no doubt affect your relationship one way or another. How parents react to their child's failure might be an even more important lesson than the one the child will learn from failure itself.

So if the lesson is to be learned properly, the parent must consider any one of the following decisions:

Box 2: Decision
Potential Decisions:
- Plan to meet with your child privately and discuss the reasons why he/she might have failed.
- Remain calm and ask your child if there is anything troubling him/her.
- Remind your child of how important his/her education is and that while one test might not be the end of the world, it could lead to a habit of giving up.
- Come to an agreement that it won't happen again.
- Make a plan to be more involved in his/her schoolwork to keep him/her motivated and on task.

The chaos addict might choose to react to initial feelings instead of taking action to help his/her child. Parents must always be considerate of and sensitive to the situation their child is in. They must do what they can to maintain the ability to see themselves in their child's shoes.

If parents take no action to help their child, the child may interpret this as a lack of care. On the other hand, if the parents are too harsh, the child may feel worthless, like an outcast in the family. Obviously, this is no condition in which to leave one's child.

Given the chaos that such a situation might lead to, let's examine the potential reactions of a parent in the case of a child experiencing failure:

Box 3: Reactions
Potential Reactions:
- Yell at the child before showing any sign of concern.
- Publicly humiliate the child by getting angry with him/her in front of his/her peers.
- Blame him/her for his/her failure.
- Refuse to listen to his/her reasons for failure.
- Make the child feel guilty about his/her participation (or lack thereof) in other activities.
- Use his/her failure as leverage for other disputes.

To avoid these kinds of reactions, parents and their children must work to maintain strong communicative ties. They must accept the situation and attempt to make it right. A disagreement is perfectly natural, but the ability to disagree without getting angry is something a parent and child must work on together. If not, chaos, rather than understanding, will gain strength in the home.

Box 4: Chaos
Potential Chaos:
- Loss of focus (at school, during activities, or while studying) due to frustration and a lack of confidence
- The parent/child relationship falters.
- The child gives up easily because he/she feels inadequate.
- A lack of trust from the parent (he/she can't trust that his/her child will study)
- The parent applies more, and possibly too much, pressure on the child.

Abuse

While parents' reactions to their child's failure in school can be extremely detrimental to the parent/child relationship, child abuse is a much more serious form of chaos. Child abuse is most often a result of too much stress.

The many other addictions that spring from a chaos addiction certainly have a tendency to add fuel to the fire, as well. Regardless of the source, abuse, whether verbal or physical, is essentially a highly emotional overreaction to tension between a parent and child. In the end, it is a wildly improper display of authority.

Imagine a parent who cannot control his/her own emotions. He/she takes out his/her anger, frustration, and feelings of inadequacy on the child. This is a situation no one asks for (and rarely does anyone know how to gain control over it, either), but just like the stresses of schoolwork, it is an all too common occurrence. But it is one that must be eliminated if any progress in the relationship is to be made. After all, how can an abusive parent be expected to tend to the emotions of his/her child, or even take care of the child at all?

When tension builds over time, like a teapot heating up, sooner or later it will burst. Short-tempered tiffs become embarrassing arguments, which become full-on yelling matches. From there, the gap between a verbal and physical fight can quickly fill.

In the hopes of spotting such occurrences before they arise, let's take a look at a scenario in which this level of hostility could surface.

Box 1: Triggers/Feelings

Triggers:
- The child disobeys his/her parent and talks back.
- The parent has a rough day at work and comes home angry.

Potential Feelings:
- Anger
- Frustration
- Betrayal
- Hatred

When a parent feels disobeyed or frustrated, it is easy for him/her to struggle to understand why the child did what he/she did. More than this, in some circles, abuse is considered a last-resort effort in parenting. When scolding and time-outs don't work, some parents feel they have no other choice but to harm their children. But parents can make the right decision after their child disobeys them. They can avoid a physical fight.

Let's look at healthier ways to manage this situation in Box 2:

Box 2: Decision
Potential Decisions:
- Create a neutral meeting ground in which to talk to the child about his/her behavior (in order to cut the tension).
- While keeping cool, the parent should ask the child why he/she deliberately disobeyed (remember to be considerate of the child's emotions, as well).
- Remind the child that honesty/integrity are important values that are always to be upheld.
- Design a plan for the child to help him/her avoid this behavior in the future.
- Make a promise to be a better model of integrity.

Abuse can be avoided but, very often, chaos is overpowering. Chaos can take a healthy, comfortable relationship and quickly create one of hazy misunderstanding, quarreling, and possibly physical abuse. In this sense, both parents and children must maintain a willingness to work through and solve problems. A resolution never comes with an argument.

So in the hopes of avoiding arguments of this sort, let's take a closer look at some of the negative reactions that could occur:

Box 3: Reactions
Potential Reactions:
- Immediately yell at the child before showing any sign of concern.
- Punish the child inappropriately by hitting him/her.
- Blame him/her for bad behavior (the parent refusing to take responsibility for his/her part in the episode).
- Make the child feel worthless.

It's easy to fall into these reactions, but they should be avoided, as they actually perpetuate chaos. They never resolve an issue. In parenting, the punishment must *always* fit the crime. Physical abuse (or even verbal abuse) *never* fits the crime. This being the case, both the parent and child alike need to work on becoming more sensitive to one another's position. It is much easier to avoid physical abuse than to stop abuse mid-stream.

In closing, let's take a long look at the specifics of this type of chaos.:

Box 4: Chaos
Potential Chaos:
- Loss of control (over emotions, behavior, and methods of parenting)
- The parent/child relationship becomes a power struggle (the parent becomes tyrannical).
- The child feels useless, alone, unwelcome, and unwanted.
- A lack of trust and respect from both the parents and the child
- The parent feels the child is useless and a relationship of hate develops.

Parents are overstressed with their lives. With the extra stresses that come from their kids, they have the potential to easily overreact with their own anger and take it out on their children. With the help of the Chaos Model, they may learn to deal with their stresses more efficiently. In the hopes of making better decisions in your own parenting, consider the facets of the following Balance Plan.

Balancing the Parent/Child Relationship

Let's now dig deeper into the above two scenarios by applying them to the Balance Plan to alleviate the relationship from chaos. With the help of this plan, you will be able to find solutions to the problems associated with childhood and parenting chaos. To begin, let's recall the steps of the Balance Plan.

Step One: List your triggers.

The two scenarios above involve the following triggers:

- The child disobeys his/her parent and talks back.
- The parent has a rough day at work and comes home angry.

> - The child fails an exam.
> - The child is overbooked or cannot manage his priorities.

Step Two: Break your triggers into two lists—one list being those triggers that you may control and the other being those that you may not.

The two scenarios resulted in two triggers that can be controlled and two that cannot. First, we will look at the triggers that can be controlled.

- A child fails an exam.

What is done is done. The child failed the exam. No amount of begging will convince the teacher to change the grade and no amount of screaming will help the child improve on his/her next exam. Remaining calm in this situation will put you more in the position of teacher and less in the role of judge. After all, even children learn from their mistakes. Teach the child how to better prepare for the next test. Don't simply judge his/her previous attempt.

- The child is overbooked or cannot manage his/her priorities.

Extracurricular involvement is perhaps just as important as schoolwork. But students soon see how difficult it is to balance the two. With a little bit of effort—and some cutting of extraneous activities—making a reasonable schedule of daily tasks lifts the stresses of a busy lifestyle.

Now, let's move on to the two triggers that cannot be controlled.

- The child disobeys his/her parent and talks back.

No one is perfect, and a child who occasionally disobeys the parent is expected. However, if the behavior becomes consistent, there is likely a problem. It is impossible to control a child's behavior, but entirely possible to mold it. Work to serve as a model for behavior, not an engineer.

- The parent has a rough day at work and comes home angry.

Perhaps the biggest part of a relationship is communication. If you come home with a chip on your shoulder and do not relate the reason, the child's feelings are likely to be buried. This can lead to the kind of stress and resentment that causes significant breakdown in a relationship.

Step Three: Identify how each trigger makes you feel.

The feelings listed below occur in our everyday lives, but when they are felt in the parent/child relationship, they tend to be much more serious. This is understandable. We are all more sensitive when a loving relationship results in chaos.

- Anger
- Frustration
- Betrayal
- Hatred
- Concern
- Fear

Step Four: Identify what each of these feelings means to you.

You are dealing with a loved one, so think very carefully before you write. But don't be afraid to be honest with yourself. It will only help your relationship.

- Anger:
- Frustration:
- Betrayal:
- Hatred:
- Concern:
- Fear:

Step Five: Determine the reactions these feelings lead to.

We are all too quick to react sometimes. But if you see yourself reacting in any of the following ways, the Balance Plan will serve as a great tool for bettering your parent/child relationship(s).

- Yell at the child before showing any sign of concern.
- Publicly humiliate the child by getting angry with him/her in front of his/her peers.

- Blame him/her for his/her failure.
- Refuse to listen to his/her reasons for failure.
- Make the child feel guilty about his/her participation in other activities.
- Use his/her failure as leverage for other disputes.
- Punish the child inappropriately or physically.
- Blame the child for his/her behavior without taking any responsibility for your role in the matter (establishing yourself as all-powerful).
- Make the child feel worthless.

Step Six: Develop a decision tree—a list of all the things you could do to make a decision rather than to react to your list of triggers.

The Chaos Model is all about making the right decision. In this case, that decision will lead to a better relationship with your child. Making a decision can sometimes be difficult, so the following is an outline of the short-term decisions you can make to improve your relationship with your child.

- Plan to meet with your child privately and discuss the reasons why he/she might have failed.
- Remain calm and ask your child if there is anything troubling him/her.
- Remind your child of how important his/her education is and that while one test might not be the end of the world, it could lead to a habit of giving up.
- Come to an agreement that it won't happen again.
- Make a plan to be more involved in his/her schoolwork to keep him/her motivated and on task.
- Create a neutral meeting ground in which to talk to the child about his/her behavior (in order to cut the tension).
- While keeping cool, the parent should ask the child why he/she deliberately disobeyed (remember to be considerate of the child's emotions, as well).
- Remind the child that honesty/integrity are important values that are always to be upheld.
- Make a promise to be a better model of integrity.

> • Design a plan for the child to help him/her avoid this behavior in the future.

The above list seems simple enough, as it contains short-term ways to alleviate chaos. But since the parent/child relationship is a long-term one, the decisions we make to better the relationship should also be long-term. Below, you will find solutions that will help the parent and child work together to reduce stress and stomp out chaos for the long term.

To reduce stress in the parent/child relationship:

• Create a plan that outlines the expectations of school, work, and the household.

How high should your child set his/her educational goals? What are the career goals? Are they healthy and attainable? What kind of work needs to get done around the house? Set up limitations for the number of activities they're involved in outside of the home. Set goals, establish rules, discuss your progress, and make sure you put it down on paper. Hold yourself accountable with a clear reference.

• Develop behavioral boundaries for school, work, and the home.

What is acceptable at school or work that is not acceptable at home, and vice versa? A parent shouldn't plan to bring his/her paperwork home and a student shouldn't be allowed to do his/her homework at the dinner table.

• Balance personal space with quality time.

It is very important that you and your child spend ample amount of time together, but being apart is just as healthy. Keep the communication open and learn each other's schedules and daily routines. You and your child can be individuals, have separate personal lives, and still have a great relationship.

• Itemize your relationship to make it more efficient.

Cut out all that isn't needed in your life and your life with your child. Work hard on your personal issues—all those issues that may cause the problems you are experiencing with your child. Don't participate in anything excessively. If you keep your life on an even keel, your child is more likely to do the same.

Step Seven: Outline the situations in your life that most commonly lead to chaos.

This chapter has covered just two scenarios in the parent/child relationship that could lead to chaos. The typical parent/child relationship is certainly more complex than that. Now is your chance to identify the situations in your life that most commonly lead to chaos.

Chaos scenarios between you and your child:

1.
2.
3.
4.
5.

Step Eight: Use the Chaos Model as a guide.

After you've identified the chaos scenarios, you may now apply them to the following model. Use this as a guide to eliminate chaos and solve the problems in your relationship.

Scenario 1:

> **Box 1: Triggers/Feelings**
> *Triggers:*
> -
> -
> -
>
> *Potential Feelings:*
> -
> -
> -
> -
> -

Box 2: Decisions
Potential Decisions:

-
-
-
-
-

Box 3: Reactions
Potential Reactions:

-
-
-
-
-

Box 4: Chaos
Potential Chaos:

-
-
-
-
-

Scenario 2:

Box 1: Triggers/Feelings
Triggers:
-
-
-

Potential Feelings:
-
-
-
-
-

Box 2: Decisions
Potential Decisions:
-
-
-
-
-

Box 3: Reactions
Potential Reactions:
-
-
-
-
-

Box 4: Chaos
Potential Chaos:
-
-
-
-
-

Scenario 3:

Box 1: Triggers/Feelings
Triggers:
-
-
-

Potential Feelings:
-
-
-
-
-

Box 2: Decisions
Potential Decisions:
-
-
-
-
-

Box 3: Reactions
Potential Reactions:
-
-
-
-
-

Box 4: Chaos
Potential Chaos:
-
-
-
-
-

Scenario 4:

Box 1: Triggers/Feelings
Triggers:
-
-
-

Potential Feelings:
-
-
-
-
-

Box 2: Decisions
Potential Decisions:
-
-
-
-
-

Box 3: Reactions
Potential Reactions:
-
-
-
-
-

Box 4: Chaos
Potential Chaos:
-
-
-
-
-

Scenario 5:

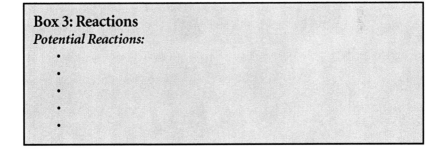

Box 1: Triggers/Feelings
Triggers:
-
-
-

Potential Feelings:
-
-
-
-
-

Box 2: Decisions
Potential Decisions:
-
-
-
-
-

Box 3: Reactions
Potential Reactions:
-
-
-
-
-

Box 4: Chaos
Potential Chaos:
-
-
-
-
-

Chapter 11

Marriage Chaos

Sticking with the theme of chaos that occurs within the home, we now move from childhood and parenting chaos to marriage chaos. People often rush into things, marry the "wrong" person, change, or just become unhappy together. We've all heard the cliché, "I was happy until I got married." Husbands and wives experience chaos in much the same fashion as a parent and child. They blame each other, get angry at one another, are dishonest, and are perhaps even disloyal.

But what sets marriage chaos apart from the parent/child relationship is that while a parent and child are often alike in many ways, a husband and wife often come from completely different backgrounds. They are often from different cultures, religions, or regions. At the very least, even if they grew up in the same town or went to the same high school, they came from different families and upbringings.

It's hard enough when two people from different backgrounds have to work together, but a married couple has to live together, raise a family together, and share their entire lives with one another. Meanwhile, in order to remain happy with one another, the couple must maintain the kind of relationship desired by both. Sometimes spouses struggle with not having time to do leisure activities on their own, and sometimes they struggle with not having enough time to spend together.

The stress of marriage can begin as early as day one. From this early point, it's up to the bride and groom to make it work. They have to compromise and communicate. They have to plan and adapt. And they have to work together on everything from daily chores to raising children. That is, if they want to lead a life devoid of chaos.

Marital Compromise

With marriage, you may find that you lose time with your family, have to give up hobbies, or even lose time for friends. As you will see, you should not have to give up everything you enjoy, but if you want to have a healthy relationship, you and your spouse will have to compromise.

Imagine a very active newlywed couple. They are excited about their new life together. The husband is a doctor and the wife is a lawyer: a perfect match of ambitious, organized, and well-rounded individuals. The wife, in her spare time, volunteers at a youth camp and plays cello in the city orchestra. The husband plays bass guitar and sings in a locally successful rock band. They are very passionate, loving, and caring individuals.

But they are in over their heads. They have no time for each other.

Let's examine Box 1 to see the triggers/feelings of such a situation.

Box 1: Triggers/Feelings
Triggers:
- The couple has no time together.
- Each spouse feels the other is too involved with hobbies to have a successful, healthy relationship.

Potential Feelings:
- Anger
- Frustration
- Distrust
- Fear (that the relationship won't work)
- Blame (the spouse for his/her involvement)

Blame and frustration are perhaps the most obvious feelings. A wife may blame her husband for being too interested in his hobby and become frustrated when he's not around. Maybe the husband feels the same about his wife. This situation leads to anxiety, anger, fear and distrust.

Despite the triggers and feelings that could occur, there are a few reasonable decisions that could be made to resolve this problem and alleviate the potential for chaos.

Box 2: Decisions
Potential Decision:
- Calmly tell your spouse that you feel you aren't spending enough time together.
- Make a list of all your activities and agree to sacrifice the ones of least importance.
- Balance your weekly schedule to include an appropriate amount of time together.
- Try to mold your individual activities into ones you can do together.)

These decisions serve as a compromise. A husband and wife can have individual hobbies, but they still have to find time to spend with each other.

But, unfortunately, when a couple is already too busy to spend time together, they can be too busy to be rational and reasonable. Box 3 outlines some of the reactions that could result from the initial triggers.

Box 3: Reactions
Potential Reactions:
- Yelling at the spouse for being selfish.
- Forcing him/her to sacrifice his/her hobbies.
- Making assumptions about the spouse's activities.
- Blaming him/her for the lack of time spent together.

These reactions are, of course, not healthy ways to deal with this situation. Regardless of how long a couple has been married, both people will still harbor the level of sensitivity and emotion that can lead to irrational, reactionary behavior. This behavior can only lead to chaos. If the couple doesn't learn to deal with their situation in a healthy way, the scenarios in Box 4 could be the result.

Box 4: Chaos
Potential Chaos:
- Arguments
- Resentment
- Physical and emotional distance
- Declining marriage
- Divorce ("We're just too different.")

The more time a couple spends apart, the more likely they are to grow apart. The husband in our scenario may come to care more about his band and the wife may come to care more about the youth camp. Regardless of where the two stand in life, if arguments and resentment are the chosen outlets for triggers/feelings, the marriage will suffer greatly.

Division of Labor

One of the most difficult parts of marriage is managing the work—and marriage, as many of us know, is a lot of work. A married couple has to balance their jobs, their kids, chores around the household, the bills, and, ideally, a social life. Both spouses can struggle to balance what they contribute to the relationship. An imbalance in the division of labor within the marriage can also create resentment and chaos.

Consider the story of Lucy, a hard-working wife and mother of two. She labors through a forty-hour workweek as a florist at her own flower shop. She wakes up at five-thirty every morning to get ready for work, get her kids ready for school, and prepare a healthy breakfast for her family before she heads off to the flower shop by 7 a.m.

She gets off work at 4 p.m., picks the kids up from the babysitter and is home by 4:30 p.m. She gets the kids started on their homework and preheats the oven for supper. She helps the children with their homework, makes the family meal, sets the table, and has dinner ready just in time for her husband to return home from his own place of business.

After dinner, she cleans up the kitchen, takes her daughter to trumpet lessons and her son to tae kwon do by 7 p.m. She runs a few errands, and then picks up both her children by 8 p.m. only to return home, get her kids ready for bed, go over the next day's schedule, and tuck the children in. It's 9:30 p.m. and she hasn't had a moment to herself. She's exhausted. Just before Lucy closes her eyes, she thinks about how tomorrow will be just like today.

All the while, Lucy's husband feels he works hard for their marriage. He does have a great job, makes a substantial amount of money to support his family, pays the bills, and takes care of the yard work on the weekends. But little does he know that his wife lays awake at night feeling underappreciated.

Lucy and her husband aren't communicating about their imbalanced work and parenting schedules. Lucy experiences several triggers/feelings as a result of the chaos in her life.

Let's examine Box 1 to see what Lucy is feeling.

Box 1: Triggers/Feelings
Triggers:
- Taking on too much responsibility in the marriage
- The suspicion that her spouse doesn't care about the family

Potential Feelings:
- Fear (that the marriage is falling apart)
- Frustration (from the husband's unwillingness to help)
- Resentment
- Jealousy (that the husband has his evenings free)
- Exhaustion
- Anger (from a lack of understanding and communication)

A lifetime of Lucy's routine isn't healthy for a person's stress level or marriage. Lucy still loves her husband, but feels he isn't doing his part. After all, a marriage is supposed to be about compromises and cooperation.

If you find yourself feeling like you are in Lucy's shoes, Box 2 highlights a few decisions you could make in your own marriage.

Box 2: Decision
Potential Decisions:
- Meet with your spouse and discuss the responsibilities of the marriage.
- Calmly explain to your spouse that you feel overworked and under-appreciated.
- Remind your spouse that marriage is about compromises and balancing the workload.

> • Reach an agreement that outlines the workload of each spouse (to prevent this situation from happening again).

These decisions may seem simple enough, but for someone stuck in a cycle of chaos, they aren't always easy. It may be much easier to keep quiet and let chaos consume your life. It may be even easier to react to the frustration and anger rather than try to compromise.

Box 3 highlights some of the potential reactions associated with this common situation:

Box 3: Reactions
Potential Reactions:
- Yell at your spouse the minute you see him/her sit down to rest.
- Blame your spouse for not doing his/her part.
- Fail to listen to your spouse.
- Make your spouse feel guilty for his/her lack of work.
- Hold in your feelings, letting them build up inside.
- React to other situations with more anger than would be normal.

If we let chaos consume our lives and our relationships, the reactions above will seem like the only outlet. A spouse who is going through what Lucy has experienced needs to be open and willing to express his/her feelings in a healthy way. If these reactions become second nature, only chaos can ensue. Let's look at Box 4, which highlights the potential chaos that can be derived from these reactions.

Box 4: Chaos
Potential Chaos:
- Loss of focus on the daily schedule and on the relationship (it might become all about the work or all about the kids)
- The relationship may reach a critical low (no communication).
- Divorce (from a lack of compromise)

> • Addictive behaviors (sleeping more, taking medications, drinking alcohol, etc.)

When a husband and wife don't share the workload, the relationship becomes more about resentment and holding back. The relationship could also shift focus. One spouse may compromise his/her marriage for the sake of the kids or his/her job. Marriage is supposed to be about a common bond. In this way, in order to avoid chaos, a couple has to seek the means to achieve balance.

Balancing the Marriage

Let's recall each of the above scenarios and insert them into the Balance Plan to see how one can alleviate the chaos in married life. The plan's purpose is to give you a clearer picture of what steps to take to avoid the unnecessary stresses and chaos associated with marriage. It will be an aide to both you and your spouse.

Step One: List your triggers.

The triggers in marriage chaos are as follows:

> • The couple has no time together.
> • Each spouse feels the other is too involved with hobbies to have a successful, healthy relationship.
> • Each spouse feels they spend too much time together.
> • One spouse takes on too much responsibility in the marriage.
> • The suspicion that the spouse doesn't care about the family

Step Two: Break your triggers into two lists—one list being those triggers that you may control and the other being those that you may not.

Let's first look at the triggers you may control.

• The couple has no time together.

Getting upset about a situation like this will do absolutely no good for you or your spouse. If you feel you don't spend enough time with your partner, talk to him/her about ways you can spend more. Agree that you must make sacrifices in order for your relationship to be successful.

- One spouse takes on too much responsibility in the marriage.

It's surprisingly easy for a husband or wife to take on the bulk of responsibility in the marriage. It isn't fair, no matter which way you look at it. An imbalance in the workload can create resentment.

Now let's look at the ones you may not control:

- Each spouse feels the other is too involved.

While it may be easy to identify that you and your spouse aren't spending enough time together, it's much harder to decide who's responsible. It's best not to blame anyone. This problem is solved by good communication skills and the willingness to compromise. Step back and take a look at your own involvement before you accuse your spouse of anything.

- Suspicion that the spouse doesn't care about the family

This is a very sensitive trigger. If a spouse suspects that the other has quit caring about the family, the approach is everything. If blame and resentment are the first reactions, it can be extremely detrimental to the family, not just the relationship. After calmly discussing this problem, one way to solve it is to balance family time and individual freedom.

Step Three: Identify how each trigger makes you feel.

- Afraid
- Frustrated
- Resentful
- Jealous
- Exhausted
- Angry
- Distrusting

Step Four: Identify what each of these feelings means to you.

- Fear:
- Frustration:
- Resentment:
- Jealousy:
- Anxiety:
- Anger:
- Distrust:

Step Five: Determine the reactions these feelings lead to.

These reactions are quite common, but here they are specific to the situation. Marriage creates a new lifestyle for most people, one they have to adapt to. Without the willingness to change and cooperate, these reactions will become even more common.

> - Yell at your spouse without warning.
> - Blame your spouse for not doing his/her part.
> - Fail to listen to your spouse.
> - Make your spouse feel guilty for his/her lack of work.
> - Hold in your feelings and let them build up inside.
> - React to other situations with more anger than would be normal.
> - Yell at your spouse for being selfish.
> - Force him/her to sacrifice his/her hobbies for your life together.
> - Make assumptions about your spouse's activities.
> - Blame him/her for the lack of time spent together.

Step Six: Develop a decision tree—a list of all the things you could do to make a decision rather than to react to your list of triggers.

The chaos model requires short-term and long-term decisions. The short-term decisions have already been stated in the above scenarios. Here's a reminder:

- Calmly tell your spouse that you feel you aren't spending enough time together.
- Make a list of all your activities and agree to sacrifice the ones of least importance.
- Balance your weekly schedule to include an appropriate amount of time together.
- Try to mold your individual activities into ones you can do together.
- Meet with your spouse and discuss the responsibilities of the marriage.
- Calmly explain to your spouse that you feel overworked and under-appreciated.
- Remind your spouse that marriage is about compromises and balancing the workload.
- Reach an agreement that outlines the workload of each spouse (to prevent this situation from happening again).

Having a successful marriage means maintaining the short-term goals and extending them into long-term ones. Here are a few ideas of what you and your spouse can do to avoid stress and to continue to grow in your life together.

To reduce stress in the marriage:

- Eliminate unnecessary individual activities.

Talk with your spouse about which activities he/she could give up for the benefit of the marriage and family. Most spouses, when reasoned with calmly, are willing to give up or cut back on the weekly card game or the monthly fishing trip.

- Find social activities that allow you to be together.

If you have to cut out activities that keep you apart, you can substitute activities that can bring you together. If you're both interested in music, combine your efforts. If you both like volunteer work, set up an organization together.

- Make a weekend cycle.

Spend the first weekend together as a family (plan day trips or have backyard games). Spend the second one apart (let the kids go out with their friends and you and your spouse go out with your own friends). Spend the third weekend together as a couple (plan a romantic outing or just hang out together). Finally, spend the last weekend together again as a family. Setting up this routine will help reopen the lines of communication and bring the family back together.

- Keep the communication levels high.

Ask your spouse if he/she approves of you joining a new book club. He/she is more likely to be happy for you than to keep you from doing it. Furthermore, even if you both have your own individual activities, remember to share your experiences with each other. Individual experiences can really help a couple get to know each other. A good relationship thrives on questions. But if you spend your whole day together, you won't have any questions to ask.

Step Seven: Outline the situations in your life that most commonly lead to chaos.

Chaos Scenarios:

1.
2.
3.
4.
5.

Step Eight: Use the Chaos Model as a guide.

Now, using the blank form below, take all of your chaos scenarios from *Step Seven* and fill in the feelings associated with them, the decisions you can make, your potential reactions, and the possible chaos. Once this form is completely filled out, it will be a great reference for you when deciding how to handle a certain situation.

Scenario 1:

Box 1: Triggers/Feelings
Triggers:
  •
  •
  •

Potential Feelings:
  •
  •
  •
  •
  •

Box 2: Decisions
Potential Decisions:
  •
  •
  •
  •
  •

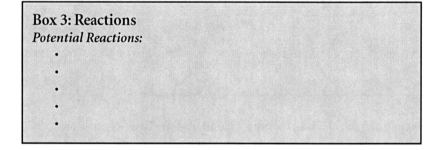

Box 3: Reactions
Potential Reactions:
  •
  •
  •
  •
  •

Box 4: Chaos
Potential Chaos:
-
-
-
-
-

Scenario 2:

Box 1: Triggers/Feelings
Triggers:
-
-
-

Potential Feelings:
-
-
-
-
-

Box 2: Decisions
Potential Decisions:
-
-
-
-
-

Box 3: Reactions
Potential Reactions:
-
-
-
-
-

Box 4: Chaos
Potential Chaos:
-
-
-
-
-

Scenario 3:

Box 1: Triggers/Feelings
Triggers:
-
-
-

Potential Feelings:
-
-
-
-
-

Box 2: Decisions
Potential Decisions:
-
-
-
-
-

Box 3: Reactions
Potential Reactions:
-
-
-
-
-

Box 4: Chaos
Potential Chaos:
-
-
-
-
-

Scenario 4:

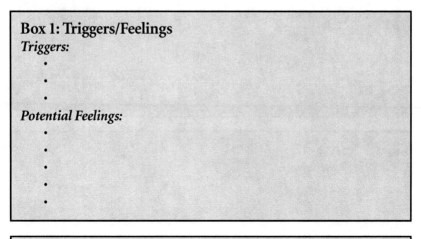

Box 1: Triggers/Feelings
Triggers:
-
-
-

Potential Feelings:
-
-
-
-
-

Box 2: Decisions
Potential Decisions:
-
-
-
-
-

Box 3: Reactions
Potential Reactions:
-
-
-
-
-

Box 4: Chaos
Potential Chaos:
-
-
-
-
-

Scenario 5:

Box 1: Triggers/Feelings
Triggers:
-
-
-

Potential Feelings:
-
-
-
-
-

Box 2: Decisions
Potential Decisions:
-
-
-
-
-

Box 3: Reactions
Potential Reactions:
-
-
-
-
-

Box 4: Chaos
Potential Chaos:
-
-
-
-
-

Chapter 12

Chaos at Work

M any of us can identify with the desire to increase our pay-grade, solidify that promotion, or achieve senior status. We can see the appeal of the corner office, to be called "boss," and to just generally have respect at work. But achieving these goals is no easy task. No one with a personal life consumed by chaos can reach these heights. In fact, if one starts to bring chaos to work, even the menial tasks can become a challenge.

We all have different personalities and can't always expect to get along with our coworkers. But a positive, reasonable attitude can make all the difference in your career. Whether you're a manager or low-level employee, you have to maintain the right attitude when dealing with other employees.

The previous few chapters have covered chaos at home, chaos between a parent and child, and chaos in the marriage. If you allow work to consume your life at home or your life with your child or spouse, your relationships outside of work will be chaotic. You will have the same result if you let your personal life affect your job. For this reason, it is important to keep your personal life and your career mutually exclusive—at least to some degree.

The workplace is no place for distraction. If your life at work is directly affected by your life outside of work, you won't be able to complete the required tasks to do your job well. But the greatest factor in determining job happiness is job success. The only way to achieve job success and get that promotion is to have the right attitude. And chaos is the antithesis of the right attitude.

Attitude

The primary reason for people not getting promoted is based on the attitude of the employee. Maybe you work overtime and do an excellent job in your field, but if you demonstrate moodiness, selfishness, and self-centeredness when working with other staff, you are not going to get the promotion. Just like on the day you came in for the interview, if you are not pleasant to work with, you aren't going to get what you want.

Imagine a young businessman, fresh out of a top-tier MBA program, who has just returned from his honeymoon. He's an intelligent, quick-witted, and charming young man. He's got everything going for him. He decides to take the next step in his business career by applying for the mid-level executive position at a nationally recognized investment firm. He knows how to dress, he's highly qualified, and he's seemingly just the right choice for the job. The investment firm hires him after the first interview and he starts a week later.

Several months down the road, his attitude seems to change. He's no longer the quick-witted and fun-to-work-with kind of manager the company had hired. There have been countless complaints from all staff, as well as some of the firm's best customers, that he has developed a poor atti-tude.

One day, his superior calls him into his office and asks him why he's acting the way he is. He tells his superior that he feels he just can't get along with his staff, he's finding it hard to accept their opinions, and they rarely agree on anything. He is now behind on his work, as a result. He feels he's let down his employees and the company. He wants to make things right, but he just keeps digging further into a hole.

The stresses and strains of a new job have greatly affected this young man's attitude. Furthermore, his inability to complete the tasks at hand has made his job even more difficult. He is experiencing several triggers and feelings in this situation.

Let's examine Box 1 of the Chaos Model to see more clearly what he is going through:

Box 1: Triggers/Feelings

Triggers:
- Your personality clashes with your coworkers'.
- Your office staff is complaining about you and your attitude.

Potential Feelings:
- Anger (at yourself for not being a good leader)
- Fear (of losing your job, that you lack experience, of losing respect)
- Guilt (for letting your coworkers down)
- Frustration
- Stress (because you're now behind on your work)

The young man feels stuck. He's in a hole that he can't get out of. The workload has piled up high, he can't seem to make decisions, and his staff seems to have lost faith in him. But if he allows these feelings to consume him, nothing will change.

Let's examine Box 2 of the model to learn some of the potential decisions you could make, were you in his shoes:

Box 2: Decision

Potential Decisions:
- Ask for help at work.
- Organize your work by making a schedule that allows you to complete it in a reasonable timeframe.
- Schedule more informal meetings with your staff to keep communication flowing.
- Accept the opinions of others rather than knocking them down.
- Find a healthy way to manage your stress (like exercising).
- Remain calm when talking to an employee about his/her mistake.

Attitude is everything. If your life is consumed by chaos, it's easy for your attitude to change for the worse. These decisions can help you take control of work-related chaos. If you don't catch it early, it's possible that you will simply react to the difficult situation.

Box 3 shows some of the potential reactions of a person in this kind of dilemma:

Box 3: Reactions
Potential Reactions:
- Yell at your staff for their mistakes.
- Pass the buck (tell your customers it's another employee's fault).
- Blame your coworkers or customers for your mistakes.
- Fail to listen to advice from coworkers or friends.
- Guilt your coworkers ("Maybe if you'd work faster, I wouldn't be so far behind").
- Allow your difficult situation to affect the lives of others.

When presented with a difficult situation, it's almost instinct to just react. But a reaction like one of the above could hinder your chances of success—not to mention the fact that you can expect chaos to ensue.

Examine Box 4 of the model to see what potential chaos could occur:

Box 4: Chaos
Potential Chaos:
- Loss of focus on work
- Loss of friends, coworkers, etc.
- A demotion at work
- Loss of your job
- Failure to complete your work
- An unhealthy addiction to work (or alcohol and other drugs)

Not everyone gets along with one another. We all have different personalities and different approaches to the task at hand. The important thing is not to let your attitude affect the work environment (especially if you are in a management position). A good leader makes all the difference, and a good leader must be patient, solve problems, and keep communication levels high.

Personal Life

This category may seem a bit strange, but it's impossible to overlook the fact that the stresses and chaos of your personal life often affect the work environment. Many employees bring their home life to work, just like many people bring their work life to the home. These situations are equally unhealthy and are bound to result in chaos. Many people need to learn to disconnect their home life the minute they step into the office.

Again, it would be unreasonable to expect someone who is going through a divorce or serious financial issue to perform at full capacity at work. But companies can't always be sympathetic if you have a history of allowing your personal life to affect your career. It's your job to prove to your employer that you can separate these two facets of your life.

Picture a young woman who's spent the past fifteen working for a research and development company. She's always been on time and has gained a vast amount of respect from her coworkers and employer. But her life at home is a much different story—it's a life she can't seem to control and it's beginning to affect her job. Her kids are struggling in school, she and her husband don't seem to get along anymore, and she's just found out that her father has prostate cancer.

She's now always running late to work or missing work altogether. She's disorganized, disoriented, and even short-tempered with her coworkers. She knows it, too, and this isn't making life any easier for her. She's fed up with her chaotic lifestyle and doesn't know how to get it back on track.

Box 1 of the Chaos Model pinpoints some of her triggers and emotions:

Box 1: Triggers/Feelings
Triggers:
- Your home life is causing you to be late to work and do your job poorly.
- The need to be successful and happy at work

Potential Feelings:
- Anxiousness
- Frustration

- Self-loathing
- Helplessness

We all want to be successful at work and that can't happen if we don't learn to manage and take control of our lives at home. There are always situations when it feels like the workload is piling up just in time for a big event at home. You have to learn to separate the two.

Box 2 below outlines a few decisions you can make when your chaotic home life begins to take over your career:

Box 2: Decisions
Potential Decisions:
- Accept that you must first manage your problems at home.
- Ask for time off from work so you can take care of your personal life.
- Be honest with your coworkers to help them understand.
- Don't make excuses; learn to take responsibility for your actions.

It is nearly impossible to be successful in the office if you allow your personal life to take over. You must first accept that there is a problem and then find ways to solve it. Don't be too brave.

Allow others to help you—otherwise you might find yourself reacting in unhealthy ways, as shown in Box 3 of the Chaos Model:

Box 3: Reactions
Potential Reactions:
- Yelling at coworkers, family, friends, etc.
- Quitting your job
- Blaming your family for your stress at work, or vice versa
- Cursing yourself

It's easy to be hard on yourself, your coworkers, or your family. If you continue to compound the problem with these quick reactions, chaos will just as quickly begin to take over your life. And when chaos consumes both your personal and professional life, you will become driven by chaos.

Box 4 of the model shows what could occur as a result of these reactions:

Box 4: Chaos
Potential Chaos:
- Loss of respect at work
- Depression
- Demotion at work
- Loss of your job

One can't expect life to be perfect. As discussed in previous chapters, balancing work and family is a difficult task, especially when presented with a troubling situation. But making the wrong decision just leads to worse conditions like losing your job or losing respect. You can learn to balance home life and work life. And you can learn to separate the two and refocus your efforts on solving problems without letting them affect other aspects of your life. All it takes is a little balance.

Balancing Work Chaos

Let's look back at our two scenarios and see how to balance them and avoid the potential for chaos at work.

Step One: List your triggers.

- Your home life is causing you to be late to work and do your job poorly.
- The need to be successful and happy at work
- Your personality clashes with your coworkers'.
- Your office staff is complaining about you and your attitude.

Step Two: Break your triggers into two lists—one list being those triggers that you may control and the other being those that you may not.

Decide which triggers you can manage. Identifying these will help you solve the ones you cannot. In these two scenarios, there are two triggers that may be controlled.

- Your home life is causing you to be late to work and perform poorly.

We all know what mornings at the office are like, and 8 a.m. typically comes earlier than most people would care for. Also, it's really hard to forget the stresses of home by the time you get to work. One problem can easily lead to another, but these two main parts of life must be separated if chaos is to be avoided.

- Your personality clashes with your coworkers'.

It's very difficult to control the personalities of your coworkers. But controlling their personalities is exactly what you shouldn't attempt to do. You have to be considerate of your differences. Know that you are not always right and that your coworkers aren't always wrong. Communication is everything, so this trigger can be a big factor in how you perform at work.

Now let's examine the two triggers that may not be controlled.:

- The need to be successful and happy at work

We all want to like our jobs. We all desire to be successful and be able to smile while on the job. Some of us treat work as work (just a way to pay the bills), but some of us take our jobs much more seriously. Both of these approaches are normal and healthy as long as they are treated appropriately.

- Your office staff is complaining about you and your attitude.

You can't control what others say about you. It's a very difficult position to be in when you feel you're surrounded by people who don't like you. It takes some mighty thick skin. But it's quite common for employees not to get along.

Step Three: Identify how each trigger makes you feel.

- Anger (at yourself for not being a good employee)
- Fear (of losing your job, that you lack experience, of losing respect)
- Guilt (for letting your employees down)
- Frustration
- Stress (because you're now behind on your work)
- Anxiousness
- Self-loathing
- Helplessness

These feelings are quite common in situations like this. It all depends on what you do with them.

Step Four: Identify what each of these feelings means to you.

- Anger:
- Fear:
- Guilt:
- Frustration:
- Stress:
- Anxiousness:
- Self-loathing:
- Helplessness:

Step Five: Determine the reactions these feelings lead to.

You might think the following reactions are to be expected. But if you see yourself reacting in the following ways, the Balance Plan will certainly help you find a healthier way to respond to chaos.

- Yell at your staff for their mistakes.
- Pass the buck (tell your customers it's another employee's fault).
- Blame your employees or customers for your mistakes.

- Fail to listen to advice from coworkers or friends.
- Guilt your coworkers ("Maybe if you'd work faster, I wouldn't be so far behind").
- Allow your difficult situation to affect the lives of others.
- Yell at coworkers, family, friends, etc.
- Quit your job.
- Blame your family for your stress at work, or vice versa.
- Curse yourself.

Step Six: Develop a decision tree—a list of all the things you could do to make a decision rather than to react to your list of triggers.

The short-term decisions have already been laid out for us in our above two scenarios. Let's look at the short-term decisions first, and then discuss the long-term ones further.

- Ask for help at work.
- Organize your work by making a schedule that allows you to complete it in a reasonable timeframe.
- Schedule more informal meetings with your staff to keep communication flowing.
- Accept the opinions of others rather than knocking them down.
- Find a healthy way to manage your stress (like exercising).
- Remain calm when talking to an employee about his/her mistake.
- Accept that you must first manage your problems at home.
- Ask for time off from work so you can take care of your personal life.
- Be honest with your coworkers to help them understand.
- Don't make excuses; learn to take responsibility for your actions.

It is easy to see that these decisions can help alleviate stress and chaos in your life. The hard part is enacting these decisions. If you approach chaos with the long term in mind, you may not have to use these short-term decisions. But look them over again and keep them in mind as you consider the long-term things you can do to reduce stress at work.

To reduce stress at work:

- Adapt to the personalities of your coworkers.

Identify what kind of employee you are and what kind of personality you have. Furthermore, be accepting of the different personalities in the room. Do not expect everyone to agree with you or approach a task in the same way. If you have a disagreement with an employee, step aside and calmly discuss the problem. Maintain an equal playing field. A disagreement is no time for a display of power.

- Resolve the stresses at home first.

Home life can be a distraction at work. But working on ways to solve your problems at home will make your problems at work seem much easier. Also, the sooner you alleviate the stress at home, the sooner you will be back on track at work. If a particularly difficult situation arises at home, call in to work and let them know about it. You may even request to take a leave of absence until the problem is solved.

- Don't procrastinate.

If you aren't good at multitasking, plan ahead to make each task a separate entity. People who fail to do this remain in a constant state of turmoil. Procrastination is never beneficial. Planning is everything. Every Monday, or the first day of every month, take an hour or two to determine what absolutely needs to get done before the week or month ends. Also, expect to be busy right away. The more active you are right away, the easier it is to get ahead and stay ahead.

- Use vacation time.

Most companies offer a certain amount of vacation time a year. When chaos takes over your work, a break is almost always a good idea. Don't take advantage of this option just for the sake of getting away, however. Reserve vacation time for when you have really hit a low. A family vacation can also help solve some of the problems at home, which may in turn solve the problems at work. Vacation is a great time to either use for yourself, to reopen the lines of communication between you and your family, or to take a break from your coworkers.

> **Step Seven: Outline the situations in your life that most commonly lead to chaos.**

Chaos scenarios:

1.
2.
3.
4.
5.

> **Step Eight: Use the Chaos Model as a guide.**

Now take the five situations in your life that most commonly lead to chaos and plug them into the Chaos Model. Once you've completed this table, study it and use what you learn to aid you whenever your life feels chaotic.

Scenario 1:

Box 1: Triggers/Feelings
Triggers:
-
-
-

Potential Feelings:
-
-
-
-
-

Box 2: Decisions
Potential Decisions:
-
-
-
-
-

Box 3: Reactions
Potential Reactions:
-
-
-
-
-

Box 4: Chaos
Potential Chaos:
-
-
-
-
-

Scenario 2:

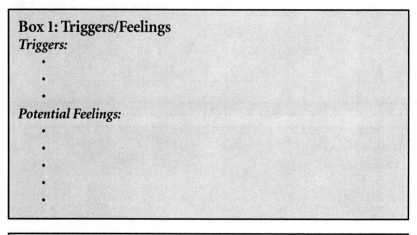

Box 1: Triggers/Feelings
Triggers:
-
-
-

Potential Feelings:
-
-
-
-
-

Box 2: Decisions
Potential Decisions:
-
-
-
-
-

Box 3: Reactions
Potential Reactions:
-
-
-
-
-

Box 4: Chaos
Potential Chaos:
-
-
-
-
-

Scenario 3:

Box 1: Triggers/Feelings
Triggers:
-
-
-

Potential Feelings:
-
-
-
-
-

Box 2: Decisions
Potential Decisions:
-
-
-
-
-

Box 3: Reactions
Potential Reactions:
-
-
-
-
-

Box 4: Chaos
Potential Chaos:
-
-
-
-
-

Scenario 4:

Box 1: Triggers/Feelings
Triggers:
-
-
-

Potential Feelings:
-
-
-
-
-

Box 2: Decisions
Potential Decisions:
-
-
-
-
-

Box 3: Reactions
Potential Reactions:
-
-
-
-
-

Box 4: Chaos
Potential Chaos:
-
-
-
-
-

Scenario 5:

Box 1: Triggers/Feelings
Triggers:
-
-
-

Potential Feelings:
-
-
-
-
-

Box 2: Decisions
Potential Decisions:
-
-
-
-

Box 3: Reactions
Potential Reactions:
-
-
-
-
-

Box 4: Chaos
Potential Chaos:
-
-
-
-
-

Chapter 13

Case Studies

Regardless of where the chaos may come from in your life, there is good news. With the use of the Chaos Model, it can be eliminated or effectively controlled. Let's take a look at several real-life people who have experienced positive outcomes after introducing the model into their own lives.

Sally D.

Sally D. is a thirty-seven-year-old woman who finds herself in an emotionally abusive marriage. Her husband was and is extremely cold to the people in his life—especially to her. Meanwhile, her daughter and two sons were rebellious and verbally abusive. This would have bothered Sally greatly, except for the fact that she had grown up in a chaotic home herself, and so had never known anything different. From the moment we first began speaking, it was clear that her life had been a rollercoaster ride full of overreactions and overstimulation.

Sally's chief complaints were depression, anxiety, and intense fears. Her symptoms included displeasure with leisure activities and constant yelling at her children, accompanied by intense rage and anger. She was experiencing an inability to concentrate and make decisions because she had extreme feelings of self-doubt. All of these feelings had escalated in the seventeen years of her marriage. She described her life as overwhelming and completely out of control. She would complain that at the end of the day, she was so exhausted that she just wanted to find a large rock and crawl under it.

In search of answers, Sally and I developed a timeline of the events that had occurred in her life. We identified patterns of behaviors that she had developed in her childhood and had continued into adulthood. She was not previously aware of these patterns because she had become accustomed to the environment that they created. She honestly thought that this was the way that life was supposed to be.

I introduced the concept of chaos addiction to her, and we began to identify the characteristics that applied to her life. She began to see how similar her childhood was compared to her life now. Understanding how her reactions to certain triggers kept her in a state of chaos was crucial to her recovery.

Sally began making decisions to create more balance in her life. Realizing that she didn't have control over many of her triggers, letting go was crucial to her recovery. It was difficult in the beginning because she continued to feel bored whenever things were calm. But in the end, by avoiding reaction to the triggers from her husband and children, Sally set an example for the whole family.

Sally now has a sense of empowerment that the decisions she makes will create more balance in her life, and she feels much better about herself. She is aware that a state of constant crisis and chaos can be both physically and emotionally damaging. And she is constantly striving to create sound, healthy decisions to avoid returning to her chaos-addicted lifestyle.

Billy A.

Billy A. is a ten-year-old whose chief problem was intense anger and rage. He would have violent temper tantrums that he could not control, both at home and at school. At times, he presented a danger to himself and others. The episodes had been occurring on the average of once a week for about four years.

Unfortunately for Billy, he remained unable to identify the causes of his anger outbursts. He always felt bad after they happened, but he believed that he had no control over his impulses.

As Billy and I talked, it became clear that his family environment was extremely chaotic, full of overstimulation and pressure. His parents were controlling high-achievers who expected much from Billy academically, perhaps too much. There was a great deal of yelling in his home.

Because of these family dynamics, many of his outbursts could be explained as an attempt to control a situation that Billy otherwise felt he had no control over. Billy was using his anger and rage to try to adjust to an environment that had all of the characteristics of a chaos-addicted lifestyle. In a sense, he was only mimicking his parents. Even at school, Billy would create his own chaos, blaming others, saying that no one liked him. In retrospect, he wasn't liked because of his own behavior.

Letting go of his triggers and focusing on making good decisions to create balance in Billy's life were key elements to stopping the anger and temper tantrums. Empowering him to make wise decisions has created a healthier lifestyle for both Billy and his parents. The whole family is now making better choices. Billy has had no outbursts in over a year because he is aware of certain triggers and now has a tool chest of decisions that create harmony and balance in his life. The need for self-sabotaging behaviors has been replaced with conscious decisions when dealing with potentially chaotic situations.

Melissa R.

Melissa R., forty-five years old, was experiencing overwhelming anxiety and chronic pain. She described her life as full of turmoil. She was in an out of control relationship, in and out of marriages, and had two rebellious children.

As she was growing up, Melissa's parents had been extremely verbally abusive and controlling. So it only stood to reason that she would behave the same way with her own spouse and children.

Melissa and I began to identify the key triggers in her family life that demonstrated that she was living her life as a chaos addict and how she was creating an environment of self-sabotage. She was unable to relax, she scheduled activities with her children that were impossible to maintain, and she constantly felt a need to control all situations, even ones that she had absolutely no control over. These behaviors were exhausting, but she continued to harbor a need to blame others or make excuses for her feelings of being overwhelmed. She would often complain of not having enough time for herself or for leisure activities.

Melissa began to understand that she often created chaotic situations because she feared the boredom that came with calm and leisure. She now strives to identify the triggers that start the cycle of chaos by making wise decisions that create balance in her life.

Scott and Tamara W.

Scott and Tamara are a married couple who once felt that their marriage of ten years was no longer fun and that they were always in a state of turmoil. Scott was always getting involved in reckless activities such as gambling, and he frequently changed jobs. He thrived on living in the fast lane. Tamara was always concerned about her appearance and was overly critical of herself. Shopping was her favorite pastime.

Scott and Tamara's lives prior to having children had been carefree and fun-filled, with many lavish trips and parties, but after having children, their lifestyle changed drastically. They could no longer maintain the frenzied pace of their former lives.

As we began to examine their current situation, it became apparent that part of their attraction to one another had been their ability to feed off of each other's chaos. Cracks in the marriage had developed because they had become bored with it after the kids arrived, and each was resentful of the other. Neither person was willing to accept responsibility for his/her own discontent. Instead, their lives had become cluttered with anger, disappointment, and blame.

We began to explore the concept that their chaotic childhoods had led them to become chaotic adults. They had learned to survive in that atmosphere, and those same survival patterns had carried over into adulthood. Their current problems with gambling, shopping, job changes, and constant relocating represented little more than a camouflage for the underlying currents of chaos in their lives. They were contributing to their own self-sabotage and feeding their appetites as chaos addicts.

After being introduced to the concept of chaos addiction, both agreed that that could be their problem, but they thought that they were powerless to stop the cycles of behavior that they had developed.

The first step was to develop a true understanding of the triggers in their lives that created certain feelings then to look at ways to change those ingrained behaviors. After they admitted that they were both at fault, they began to explore how both of them were contributing to the downfall of their marriage.

We talked about how it was okay to feel some amount of boredom, and relaxing is not a crime. Feeling all right when nothing is going on is part of balance in life; creating turmoil where none exists would only lead them back to their chaos-addicted lives. As Scott and Tamara began to apply these concepts at home, they found new joy in their marriage and their lives as parents.

The four stories listed above are about real people. These people all shared two things in common: The first is that they came to me with a problem—one that could be summed up and defined with a deeper understanding of chaos addiction. And the second is that they are now well on their way to solving the problem, thanks to the keen application of the Chaos Model in their lives. All of them have begun to work on Balance Plans. And all of them are now feeling as if they have more control over the things they may control and more willingness to let go of the things they can't.

If the people involved in these four stories can overcome their chaos addictions, so can you. Follow the model as closely as they have, and even the deepest of addictions can be overcome.

Chapter 14

Conclusion

Tom Marlin is still considered by many to be a laidback guy. His friends still tend to count on him for advice, problem solving, and fun. But these days, even his wife and secretary would agree on these qualities. Thanks to Tom's concentration on the Chaos Model, his own unique Balance Plan, and the healthy dose of organizational skills that the two tools give him, he is no longer referred to as "the master of disaster." No longer does Tom have a tendency to lose things at the wrong time. More importantly, no longer does Tom take it out on his wife or secretary whenever something goes wrong. It might seem like a trivial change in the end—overcoming a tendency to misplace things and yell—but to Tom's wife and secretary, the difference is astronomical. To them, Tom is a much-improved entrepreneur and husband.

Nancy Garson's seeming inability to prepare for travel is a thing of the past, as well. As she found, her complete lack of foresight was owed mostly to a cluttered mind. And how did her mind get so cluttered? Her constant work and personal obligations certainly did not help. These days, thanks to her Balance Plan, she finds keeping a clear head to be a far easier proposition. And you know what? She doesn't forget her cell phone charger on vacation anymore.

Real estate agent Barry Janus is still the king of storytelling—only now, his stories don't all end in disaster or embarrassment. Thanks to the Chaos Model, he no longer bumbles through life like a chicken with its head cut off. He no longer assumes control over things that cannot be controlled. And he no longer promises things he simply cannot be expected to deliver.

Melissa Lowder is now the top saleswoman in her office. Why is this? Because she has stopped making excuses for her poorer sales months and has stopped letting her social and family life get in the way of her career. With the Balance Plan, she has learned how to keep her home life at home and, just as importantly, her work life at work. These days, her really good sales months are far more frequent and her slumps are far more rare. And in the end, not only is her life happier, but her bank account is healthier, as well.

This country and this culture are locked in a struggle with chaos. It has worked its way so deeply into our collective consciousness that it is sometimes difficult to imagine a scenario in which is is beaten. But I see those scenarios every day in my office. More and more, my clients come to me with smiles on their faces, knowing that they are making progress toward balance, knowing that they have managed to tear themselves away from the unnecessary strictures and stressors of this "all work and no play" society.

For them, it has been no easy task. Modern life makes it very difficult to break the pattern of chaos. For parents, there is often too much that "must be done" for twenty-four hours to cover. For couples, there are far too many distractions and hindrances to a healthy relationship. For children, the negative influences and quick fixes for entertainment make the idea of leading a balanced life seem nearly impossible.

Rest assured that no one—no matter how tough it may seem or how deep the chaos addiction—is beyond saving. People in this country beat addiction of every kind, every day. And if drug or alcohol addictions may be overcome, so, too, may their underlying source.

In this book, you have read many stories and have been exposed to many different forms of chaos. Some of these stories have been true-life accounts and some have been allegories to make a point about common forms of chaos addiction. Through their lessons, you have learned that decisions make for the route to balance while reactions— their simpler and more common cousins—always lead directly to more chaos and stress. More importantly, you have learned that there is an outlet for chaos and there is a solution to even the most deeply rooted of addictions.

The Chaos Model may seem simple or even obvious at first glance, but there is no denying its power. Time after time, people who have come into my office to learn about the model and apply it to their lives have seen tremendous success. The sooner they begin to consider the model whenever they encounter a new and problematic trigger or feeling, the sooner they begin their road to overcoming addiction. The Chaos Model, in this way, is more than just four little boxes. It is the path to a lifestyle that many of us crave but do not know how to achieve. It is the path out of the depths of chaos.

Its simplicity does not mean that beating a chaos addiction is simple, however. Overcoming addiction and working toward a balanced life is a difficult and often long-term process. Old habits die hard, as they say. More than that, they tend to return far more quickly and easily than they were discarded. The recovering chaos addict must therefore be ever diligent and vigilant. The people who manage this task will begin to build new patterns into their lives—and those patterns will lead to a greater sense of harmony in relationships, at home, and at work. Children, too, can and will learn by the examples set by their parents. Regardless of the age of the child living at home, a positive change in behavior and lifestyle by the parent is likely to lead to a positive change in the behavior and lifestyle of the child.

The dozens of stories presented in this book represent proof that chaos addiction, with the right tools at hand, is a problem that *can* be solved. Learn to apply the Chaos Model and Balance Plan to your own life and you will find the balance and harmony that has seemed to elude you for so long. You can and will overcome.

Endnotes

1 http://www.cdc.gov/mmwr/preview/mmwrhtml/mm5434a2.htm

2 Ibid.

3 http://www.ndvh.org/educate/abuse_in_america.html

4 http://www.childhelp.org/resources/learning-center/statistics

5 http://www.harrisinteractive.com/news/newsletters/k12news/HI_
   TrendsTudes_2007_v06_i03.pdf

6 http://pediatrics.aappublications.org/cgi/reprint/122/2/306?maxto
   show=&HITS=10&hits=10&RESULTFORMAT=&fulltext=graph
   ic+violence&andorexactfulltext=and&searchid=1&FIRSTINDEX
   =0&sortspec=relevance&resourcetype=HWCIT

LaVergne, TN USA
17 June 2010
186433LV00004B/34/P